telling the truth:

Letters and Reflective Essays

Thaddeus (Ted) Perzanowski

Library of Congress Control Number: 2022916324

ISBN: 979-8-218-43557-8

www.talktotedinc.com

To Lawrence Zimmer

with gratitude beyond words

for the life, values, and wisdom

with which he has enriched me

and for the marriage that we've shared

since 1986.

Contents

First Letter: An Opening Letter to You   3

Reflective Essays

1. Telling the Truth and No More Pretending   9
2. The Baffling Pain of Childhood   21
3. Struggle versus Challenge   31
4. As Basic as One, Two, Three   41
5. Unpacking and Weeding   51
6. Navigation/Survival Strategies   61
7. Literal Language Telling the Truth   67
8. "Bad" Words   79
9. The Kaleidoscope of Three-Dimensional Living   113
10. A Mission of Loyalty   117

More Letters

11. To Life Partners   127
12. To Parents   139
13. To Young People   147
14. To Resistors   153
15. To Helping Professionals   159

Last Letter: A Closing Letter to You   167

Appendix A: Authors of and Resources for Additional Reading   175

Appendix B: Meditate through Writing Every Week of the Year   177

First Letter

An Opening Letter to You

Dear Readers:

So many people have written before me with insights into the human condition that have been intriguing, challenging, impactful, and inspiring for me personally, for you, and for countless others. They have made valuable contributions with their work so that each of us can understand ourself better and arrive at greater personal peace.

The philosophers, poets, psychologists, reflective writers, social workers, and theologians who have most influenced me include (in alphabetical order): Peter Breggin, the CDC (the United States Centers for Disease Control) and their ACEs (Adverse Childhood Experiences) research, Jean Jenson, Alice Miller, Martin Miller, Mary Oliver, M. Scott Peck, Robert Whitaker, and coauthors Oprah Winfrey and Bruce Perry. Someone who hasn't written but has contributed extensively to her clients and colleagues through her private practice is Patricia Campion, PsyD. Each of these sources has brought valuable perspective to the world and to me.

One person is pre-eminent among these sources, although not perfection personified: Alice Miller. While we all want to be fair about how our parents and families of origin enriched us growing up, Alice Miller invites us to be fair to ourselves in an additional and very specific way: **by letting ourselves see, know, and feel the truth of the less-than-enriching impacts of parents and family members on us, the impacts of the baffling experiences we navigated as children, and the often minimized fact that these baffling experiences maintain—consciously or not—a lifelong and even intrusive presence with us.**

Some of the impacts on us from our childhood experience of life (pre-birth through 18 years old, primarily during our single digit ages) are positive, some are disruptive, and they all last a lifetime.

However, it was the collection of baffling moments from our childhood experience of life that led us to unconsciously craft truly creative strategies to navigate and survive these counterproductive impacts on us from a parent and family members. These are the experiences that were hurtful, confusing, frightening, and more, for the child we each were.

Notes

These negative impacts were truly baffling for the children we once were, and the strategies we crafted in childhood to navigate them stay active in us far longer than is helpful or productive for the lives we want to live. These old, unconscious strategies may serve us well from time to time once we are no longer children, but they routinely become more counterproductive than productive as our lives progress.

The influence of the impactful contributors I have referenced in this opening letter will be woven throughout the letters and essays that I am sharing with you. While I will not often be quoting these contributors, I will list them again as "Authors of and Resources for Additional Reading" at the conclusion of this book. Neither will I be providing data from studies but, instead, encourage you to seek out additional details of interest on your own.

What I will be doing, however, is sharing the perspectives—gained through more than four decades of my professional career—that have come to most define the work I have been privileged to do with my clients, people who have taught me so much about life and who have humbled me with the opportunity to be of service to them. I offer the perspectives in this collection of letters and reflective essays in tribute to them and as the contributions of what Alice Miller calls an "Enlightened Witness" or an "Informed Companion," which I have tried to be in the work I have done across my lifetime.

Please note:

- I am not a licensed professional counselor.
- I am not a licensed clinical professional counselor.
- I am not a licensed therapist nor licensed in any profession.
- I am not a physician, doctor, or medical practitioner.

Who I am is someone with a career built on my undergraduate degree in Philosophy, my graduate degree in Divinity (a graduate program with a heavy concentration in helping skills that included counseling and social justice principles and practices), and seven years studying with Alice Miller's one-time protégé Jean Jenson.

Within a variety of professional settings, I have been providing what I believe to be an effective alternative to counseling and psychotherapy for individuals, couples, and families. My goals in life personally, socially, and professionally have been to provide

Notes

experiences that facilitate someone feeling cared for, good about themself, human, and connected to self and others.

The letters and reflective essays that I am sharing with you are my attempt to do the same via writing, and by doing so, bring a clarified simplicity to the responsibility of knowing oneself—the core responsibility in life for each person, a brave responsibility indeed to fulfill—and to the longed-for wish that almost all of us share: to know as much peace as possible in our minds, hearts, and bodies.

These pages are offered as personal reflections from me that may elicit personal reflections from within you about you. You have already seen the space for your own notes on these first pages and will find the same throughout the book.

It will be most beneficial if you read this book from beginning to end—rather than starting with a section somewhere within the book—because the sections build upon each other. You can always return to reread sections of specific interest at another time.

Please note: Within this collection of letters and essays, I will make comments about the ongoing and prevalent use of psychotropic or emotion-focused medication. As I do so, it is by no means to imply that, if someone is using such medications, they should suddenly discontinue their use. Any shift off even one of these medications has to be accomplished with the oversight help of a medical or psychiatric professional. These medications are that powerful—even those which have come to be so commonplace and in wide use.

Thank you for investing your time and energy in what you are about to read. My wish is that you find some degree of personal benefit in what I am sharing. However, this may not be an easy read for you because you will be asked to think through a lot. Read whatever amount will feel right for you at any given time. Let yourself think and feel in the ways that these pages are intended to facilitate. Take notes, underline, circle, and highlight freely as you go.

And take your time. Take your time.

Notes

A heartfelt "Thank You" to those who served as reviewers of this work:

JB, MB, PB, MC, PC,
LE, RE, AF, DF, MF,
BK, TR, KS, PS,
JT, LW, and LZ.

A special thank you to Catherine Friel, Lorie DeWorken, and Larry Butler for their editing services, without whom I may have a missed a punctuation or two.

Thank you as well to the artist Elizabeth Harper of *Lady E Photography,* who skillfully created the artwork in this book: kaleidoscopic, photographic images of homes, apartment buildings, gardens, and other locations in Michigan City, Indiana, and Chicago, Illinois.

Thank you to each of these people for their contributions to the spirit and content of these pages.

Take care.

Ted

Notes

Reflective Essays

1. Telling the Truth and No More Pretending

There are many good people—very talented and genuinely well-intentioned—who serve clients and patients in the world of mental health, self-ownership, and personal growth. However, I fear that the medicalization of personal emotional issues through diagnoses, labels, categorizations, and medications is keeping far too many service providers from actually serving their clients and patients in the most helpful of ways.

I am concerned, in fact distressed, about what I believe to be the unintentional damage done to so many by the world of psychology and psychiatry. The most skilled therapists, psychologists, clinical social workers, and psychiatrists are those who know that emotional struggling is not an illness. It's a lack of emotional ease, a dis-ease, which intrudes on someone's life. It is residue from bafflements accumulated extensively during one's early life and even passed on multi-generationally. It is an ongoing unsettledness from the ways that a parent and families of origin can leave individuals feeling about themself, about the world, about life.

Often this emotional struggling, dis-ease, unsettledness, is reflected within the body. We are most familiar with this being true about tears, headaches, gastro-intestinal issues, and changes to hair color. Each person's body cooperates in its own way as a storehouse—and sometimes as a megaphone—to give light to the difficult truths of a person's emotional life history. Any type of current-day *struggling* has roots to varying degrees in the troubling unsettledness and emotional dis-ease present in the *earliest years* of one's life.

The phrase *first impressions are lasting* is truer than we've ever believed it to be regarding how our first negative impressions of ourself, the world, and life can flare up and be actively present now and again across our lives. However, no one has to stay a hostage of these first negative impressions of self, the world, and life without some relief. Our committed exploration of the less-than-happy dimensions of the truth of our early life will be the ongoing solution to this hostage situation.

During the years when we are children, every parent (often other family members as well) is responsible for making sure that children entrusted to their care learn how to live effectively in the world and come to understand life. However, the most important job of a parent is to ensure that each child feels good about themself because they feel safe in the world, peaceful and confident being who they are—and as a result—feels treasured.

Notes

The most important job of a parent is to ensure that each child feels good about themself because they feel safe in the world, peaceful and confident being who they are— and as a result—feels treasured.

This important task does not mean coddling a child. Guidance regarding appropriate behavior, the teaching of personal responsibility on many levels, and coaching regarding effective interactions with others are all needs a child has while developing as the person they are. It is each parent's responsibility to fulfill these needs.

However, appropriate respect for, confidence in, comfort with, and pride regarding oneself are needs that are just as important for a child—if not the most important needs of a child—because, if a child can relate to themselves in these positive, healthy ways, it will set the tone for how each child interacts not only with themself but also with other people, with the world, and with life itself.

In many households there is far too much focus on a child's behavior and far too little focus given to a child's self-identity. This results in a significantly impacting lack of conscious effort by parents to genuinely know each of their children. As a parent spends time with their child and gets to know them, the child is introduced to themself by what they see on a parent's face and in their parent's eyes, what they hear in a parent's voice, what they feel from a parent's touch.

The child is introduced to themself by what they see on a parent's face and in their parent's eyes, what they hear in a parent's voice, what they feel from a parent's touch.

As a parent comes to know their child, they can then fulfill that most important job of making sure that their child feels good about themself because they feel safe in the world, peaceful and confident about themself, and treasured. Nothing means more to a child than to experience a parent and members of the family (nuclear and extended) wanting to genuinely know them, spend time with them, have the child in their lives, and want to be in the child's life.

Notes

However, when who the child is—how the child thinks and feels, what the child voices, what the child needs physically *and* emotionally while dependent on their caregivers—is not given focus and genuine human interest, the child *unconsciously but impactfully* assumes the only things they can assume because they are only a child: either that who they are as a person is not important or at least much less important than their behaviors.

This experience fosters a belief, whether genuinely true or not, that they are of little or perhaps no interest to those closest to them. It becomes a presumption which holds the child hostage, and eventually the adult, too, and has a powerfully negative impact on the direction and experience of their life.

The material things that a parent purchases for a child include housing, clothing, food, education, medical care, toys, financial support for extra-curricular activities such as sports or something within the world of the arts, perhaps some educational or recreational travel. If these are given more importance by a parent than those things the parent is responsible for providing their child that don't cost a penny—the child's feeling good about and at home with themselves, safe in the world, peaceful and self-confident, valued, interesting, liked, and treasured—then the parent's most important responsibilities for their child are not met. The level of bafflement this causes is profound for the child and has a forever impact that reveals itself across a lifetime.

When *who I am* is less important to a parent than *how I behave*, when what a parent provides a child financially is more important than what the parent could provide emotionally from their minds and hearts at no financial cost to them, there could be nothing sadder, more confusing, and more self-esteem killing for a child.

> *When who I am is less important than how I behave,*
> *when what is provided financially is more important than*
> *what could be provided emotionally at no financial cost,*
> *there could be nothing sadder for a child.*

How tragic that a child would have to unconsciously work so hard every day to navigate through such dissonance.

Every one-year-old knows what happens to anything not important and of no value in the house. It's either not cared for, not given any notice, put into storage somewhere, or

---

Notes

even thrown out. The discarded item could be an old lawn chair, an old sweater, the last plate in an old set of dishes. This is what the child sees and then believes about things and, by default, about people—which would then include the child themself.

If a child feels worthless, of little interest, of little value, even though this may not be the conscious intent of a parent or of anyone else in the household, a child could live in constant fear—usually unconscious fear—of being disregarded and perhaps even thrown out. And what if the child really is seen as worthless by a parent because of the burden or intrusion the child is to their parent or other family members? Stunning. Chilling. So very sad.

These first impressions of being oneself, of being alive, would then most certainly start the child living on varying degrees of yellow, orange, and maybe even red alert at all times. A critical question presented here *from the mind, heart, and perspective of a child* is this: Why wouldn't a child live on yellow, orange, or red alert when being of little interest, not cared for, and possibly thrown out is a daily, unconscious danger alive in the mind and heart of that child?

Being afraid is then the context in which the child starts living their life. Whether conscious of it or not, the child is likely living each day with one or more of these undercurrents to their existence:

- afraid they're not of value;
- afraid they're not safe physically, sexually, emotionally;
- afraid they don't belong and don't know how to belong;
- afraid they're not doing something right—doing something wrong—just by being alive; and
- afraid their parents don't love them—or even like them.

If these fears are the reality that is yours to navigate and survive as a child, then being afraid unconsciously becomes a default second nature or mode of operation. Everything you do is to survive. You navigate life as a frightening reality and can give no attention or energy in childhood to feeling peaceful and confident about who you are.

What takes precedence for you—and energy from you—are navigating and surviving the experiences of a parent and family members which are baffling—and for the child you were—perhaps terrifying.

Notes

Sometimes this survival mode leads a child to unconsciously be overly self-protective. Or a child can become contrary or combative because they are working so hard to stay safe from what frightens or even terrifies them. Sometimes a child goes into overdrive pleasing and fixing things in order to secure a place of safety, to earn a place of importance, because it's only this overdrive that will keep the child from being of no interest, not noticed, uncared for, or thrown away.

Whatever is unconsciously crafted for surviving and navigating any baffling unsettledness in childhood becomes the norm for living that is then followed—also unconsciously—for years. The norm should be feeling peaceful and confident with yourself in what should be the safest place in the world: with your parent or parents, with your family, in your home. But that gets put *on hold* if your daily task becomes surviving the reality of your childhood that instinctively to you doesn't make sense.

This haunting unsettledness that so many of us experienced when we were children—whether we experienced this unsettledness consciously or not—is because of how parents and family members disregarded and thus hurtfully treated us—knowingly or not—when we were children.

In some cases, this disregard and hurtful treatment was conscious and malicious. In so many other cases, it was not. However, a lack of awareness on the part of those on whom we depended for care and safety—physical, sexual, and emotional—makes their disregard and hurtful treatment just as negatively impactful as anything done intentionally. It's a sad truth that many parents never question their impact on a child entrusted to their care or, at best, give it little consideration.

> *It's a sad truth that many parents never question their impact on a child entrusted to their care or, at best, give it little consideration.*

The child's reality starts for them *in utero*, that is, what the baby senses about their parent or parents, how a parent feels about the baby on the way, how a parent interacts with their partner or with whomever. "Am I really wanted? Will I be safe?" It happens while a baby is flat on their back in the crib, meeting their parent(s) from there. This search for approval from a parent continues for the child—sometimes throughout life.

Notes

What a parent feels about their child and who they see their child to be is conveyed in the most natural yet unconscious of ways: by the look on the parent's face, by the tone of their voice, and by the quality of their touch. If these are less-than-positive experiences for the child, the child still receives a sense of themself from that parent, but a destructive sense of self and one that is baffling and terrifying beyond words: doubt about their intrinsic value as a human being.

This instilled self-doubt is a very real experience and becomes a false and unjust sense of self for the child. Each of us will live and feel throughout life as a parent and family members made us live and feel in childhood *until our awareness presents the opportunity to be otherwise* in whatever areas of life such shifts would benefit us.

It's only by the skill of ongoing self-awareness that the original sense of self can be adjusted for the better. Recalibration through self-awareness, however, is not a one-and-done. It will most likely have to happen to some degree *every day* of a person's life. This demonstrates how strong the impact is from impressions a child receives about themself from a parent. This constant process of recalibration is why it's so important that each person keep their emotional self-awareness limber and agile.

It could be that a child receives a false and unjust sense of themself because of the disregard and hurtful treatment from another family member. Even this impact, however, gets rooted back to parents if a parent allows the child to be disregarded and treated poorly by someone in the family while the parent does nothing to protect the child from an assaulter (physical, sexual, emotional) who might be the other parent, a sibling, grandparent, aunt, uncle, cousin, neighbor, or even schoolmate.

Children can unfairly and unjustly begin to feel any number of false messages, for example, that they are bad, stupid, worthless, not attractive, not interesting. It becomes how a child then regards and treats themself, what they then believe about themself. These false messages become the child's self-definition.

Until someone pauses to learn the roots of how and why they experience life and themself as they do, they will continue living—thinking, feeling, and acting—"like the child I once was"—LTCIOW. There may be an adult costume to it all, but without *conscious awareness*, adults continue living—thinking, feeling, and acting—"like the child I once was" (LTCIOW).

Notes

> *Without conscious awareness, adults continue living*
> *—thinking, feeling, and acting—*
> *"like the child I once was" (LTCIOW).*

This is true regarding what flows well in our life as well as where we struggle in life. However, it's only by our conscious awareness throughout life that we can adjust and manage any early life negative programming of how to regard and treat ourself and experience life. We, of course, want to maintain what's productive, and we also want to facilitate the recalibration of what isn't productive. By doing so we can live the life that is truly ours to live and be the person that it's our birthright to be.

The invitation to each of us is that we support each other in the sincerest and most effective of ways by telling the truth. The biggest truth, the most dismissed, overlooked, and brushed off truth, the most underrated, undervalued, underreported, and undermined truth, and at times the most joked-about truth is this: any emotional bafflement and turmoil experienced in childhood because of how a child is regarded and treated by a parent and family members:

- registers deeply;

- has a lifelong impact because it is among our first impressions of ourself, of the world, and of life itself; and

- requires a lifelong vigilance and effort to counteract the recurring intrusion (as one client put it) of the "magnitude of its [childhood's] impact" on our lives.

> *Any emotional bafflement and turmoil experienced in childhood*
> *because of how a child is regarded and treated by a parent and*
> *family members registers deeply and has a lifelong impact.*

As was noted earlier, although we have applied the saying *first impressions are lasting* in off-handed conversation, this statement is completely true regarding how a child is regarded and treated.

Regarding early life impressions, we seldom dismiss the good impacts from parents and families. Kindness toward others, work ethic, financial responsibility, cooking skills,

---

Notes

and more are all positive contributions to our life. We have routinely believed that such good done by a parent would and should far outweigh the things that left a child unsettled and baffled.

However, we've all had the experience of having a wonderful day, and then something happens around 4:30 in the afternoon and the day's "wonderfulness" is gone. Something happens like a physical accident, a harsh e-mail from a boss, or an argument with a spouse or child. The goodness of a day can be flooded out in an instant.

Example. A couple who shared a love of history took a week-long vacation to Washington, D.C. They thoroughly enjoyed visiting the many buildings of the Smithsonian Institution. The tours of the United States Capitol and White House, which their home district's member in the House of Representatives arranged for them, were special highlights. Their visits to the many memorials were moving for them both. They experienced these days as being truly awesome.

Then, when they were finished packing and ready to check out of their hotel and take a taxi to the airport, they heard sirens and more sirens. They turned on the TV. It was the morning of September 11, 2001. They would not be traveling home that day.

After a wonderful week in the capital city of the United States, which day do you think most colors what had otherwise been a wonderful trip? It was the day of baffling unsettledness—and in this case terror, too.

The dynamic this couple experienced is true for every child. Even if baffling unsettledness happens for a child just once, the impact is forever. However, baffling unsettledness for a child was most likely not a one-time event.

So much can be given to a child, but all that's provided doesn't act as white-out for unsettling bafflements that leave a child unconsciously asking why something just happened that made no sense. Perhaps because a parent turns from kind to giving-the-silent-treatment in a matter of seconds, the child wonders "What just happened? When will this happen again?" A child can't process these experiences *because they are only a child*. The experiences get stored within for unpacking at another time.

Along the way in life, what was once stored within by the child starts to reveal itself. This revealing is intrusive and disruptive. Be it during later childhood, the teenage

Notes

years, young adulthood, or adulthood, the baffling emotional turmoil and unnecessary hurts that a child filed away reappear.

These were times when a child was made to feel sad, worthless, desperate, disrespected, perhaps unsafe or even terrified physically, sexually, or emotionally—even *in utero*—by the very people with whom they presumed in their heart of hearts they would be the safest and most genuinely treasured, that is, by a parent and family members.

Specifically, regarding a child being made to feel unsafe sexually (disrespected, worthless, terrified), this does not result only from actual physical harm or violation. Even inappropriate looks, attitudes, words, creepiness, and jokes can cause a child to feel threatened and unsafe sexually.

There is a nearly universal version of the Judeo-Christian commandment "Honor Your Father and Mother" within religious, ethnic, and national cultures or within any societal philosophy we might name. However, we have counterproductively and destructively downplayed the lifelong impact of baffling words, actions, looks, attitudes, and silences most especially from parents—but also from other members of our families—that we experienced when we were children.

The fine print that seems to have been attached with invisible ink to versions of "Honor Your Father and Mother" is that if you were honest about any negative impacts on you by a parent, you would be dishonoring that parent. Honoring and honesty are not mutually exclusive. We can be honest about any less-than-positive impact on us by a parent or family member without dishonoring anyone. The honor—when earned and therefore deserved—is due them. The honesty is due us.

Most cultures of the world—secular or religious—are parent protection cultures, which is why there are various versions of "Honor Your Father and Mother" across the globe. When looking at just the Judeo-Christian Ten Commandments, it's quite amazing that millennia ago "Honor Your Father and Mother" made it into the Top Ten, but "Treasure Your Children" did not.

> *When looking at just the Judeo-Christian Ten Commandments, it's quite amazing that millennia ago "Honor Your Father and Mother" made it into the Top Ten, but "Treasure Your Children" did not.*

Notes

In the New Testament of The Bible, Jesus said that anyone doing harm to any of the "little ones" should tie a millstone around their neck and drown themself in the sea (Luke 17:2). Although this directive from Jesus gives pointed focus to how children should not be disregarded or poorly treated, few people have ever heard a sermon or homily about this passage.

Any harm done to a child by a caregiver—be the harm physical, sexual, or emotional, intentional or not—is baffling beyond words to a child because it brings up for the child the terrifying and usually unconscious awareness of not being valued, of not being treasured, by their caregivers. Not treasured by a caregiver = not safe. Period. Not feeling safe with and treasured by a parent and other family members is true trauma for a child, and it carries a lifelong impact.

Being honest about a parent's negative impact on us is not easy to do. However, when we are bravely honest about it, two things happen:

1. We end up owning ourself and managing our life better and better each day.

2. We eventually ask ourself questions about why a parent regarded and treated us as they did, come to understand that parent in a new way, and experience a new compassion for a parent's suffering in their own early life—and maybe even the suffering of previous generations within our family system—which have traveled downstream to us.

This is not to give a parent a pass on any disregard and hurtful treatment of us. These impacts have been made. However, with new and honest awareness we can manage our life better. We can also know a parent better than ever—be they alive or dead—perhaps better than anyone in the world has ever known them.

As human beings we are instinctively wired to believe that, when someone brings us into their life, into their home, into the world, they will welcome us, value us, want to know us, enjoy what they see in us, and do everything they can so that we feel safe physically, sexually, and emotionally—in short, assure that we feel treasured.

When during childhood we experienced something contrary to these presumptions, the bafflements of these experiences were alarming, confusing, often frightening, and even terrifying for the child we once were. We knew something was off. A little off or

---

Notes

terribly off makes no difference. In the constellation of that world of parent and family, something was off. We didn't know what to say or do about it. We were children.

In fact, in so many households saying something about any of this was not only discouraged, but it was also forbidden and could bring some form of punishment if we didn't comply by staying silent. Sometimes we forbade ourself from giving voice to our bafflement or hurt because we didn't want to break the gag order blatantly or subtly imposed within our family, or we didn't want to think of ourself as a bad person because of what we were thinking or feeling about a parent or family member, or we didn't want to hurt anyone's feelings.

No child has the skills of emotional calculus to understand the confusing and frightening components of the dynamic in which they are living. So, each of us did the only thing we could do with something we didn't know how to understand or handle. We put it in the only place we had to put it: within ourself. And none of it went anywhere. This unconscious awareness—of the events we didn't know how to handle and the associated emotions for which we didn't have the tools to process—has been sitting there within us our whole life whether we are ten, twenty, or eighty years old.

It is critically important to discontinue the thinking that being honest about the less-than-wonderful impacts of a parent on us will keep us from giving them whatever honor is their due. It's time for *telling the truth* about the impacts of childhood on each of us. It's time for *no more pretending* that the less-than-positive experiences of self, the world, and life given by a parent or family member when we were children—of whatever age— didn't impact and don't continue to impact us as we proceed with living our life.

In fact, the baffling impacts of parents on children can truly be called *traumatic* for a child because these impacts are too much for the child to bear. To survive them and move forward, the child hides them, camouflages them. Two common examples of camouflaging are when we think regarding a parent's behaviors, "Oh, it's no big deal," or "That's just how they are."

Unless these hidden and camouflaged negative impacts are uncovered and processed at some point—a little bit more with each step through life—they will cause untold harm and repeated sabotaging of a person's birthright: the personal confidence and peace of feeling good about themself that each person deserves to feel. The ongoing hiding and camouflaging of these negative impacts during childhood drive the trauma even more

---

Notes

forcefully into storage within a child, and the trauma remains there within the adult we each become.

Yes, even a good parent can baffle a child. If something happens out of the child's ordinarily supportive experience of a parent, this is a baffling hit, an impactful hit. If a parent realizes this, they can help the child realize it too, and put what was so out of the ordinary back into perspective, lessening the threat to the child's self-confidence, safety, and peace.

Parents do not remain the most important people in our lives. However, they forever remain the most impactful. A client in their late twenties once asked me, "Do you mean that whatever happens to us in childhood rides with us all the way through?" And I said, "Yes."

> *Our parents do not remain the most important people in our lives.*
> *However, they forever remain the most impactful.*
> *A client in their late twenties once asked me,*
> *"Do you mean that whatever happens to us in childhood*
> *rides with us all the way through?"*
> *And I said, "Yes."*

Someone in their eighties expressed this truth in a different way: "Some things just stay with us forever."

Notes

2. The Baffling Pain of Childhood

There are several ways to describe what so many of us unconsciously did with our life experiences during childhood that we didn't have the skills to make sense of or manage. Here are some metaphorical descriptions for how we stored the perplexing, hurtful, and even terrifying experiences of childhood—all of these emotionally traumatic for a child—both the content of these experiences and the emotions associated with them:

- filing them in invisible file cabinets within us;
- archiving them in the most distant corners of our emotional attic, basement, closet; and
- flash freezing them—locking them in time—in cold storage within us.

These are all metaphors for how childhood bafflements get stored in our subconscious. What might some of these experiences have been? They include:

- a parent, sibling, or other family member being seriously ill;
- a parent, sibling, or other family member attempting to take their own life;
- the death of a parent, sibling, or someone else in one's inner circle—including the death of a twin in utero;
- active arguments or perhaps chilly distance between two parents;
- "prison warden" behavior on the part of a parent including harsh tones in communication and sometimes physical assaults under the guise of discipline;
- erratic behavior of a parent due to inappropriate use of alcohol, drugs, or anything else that could alter a parent's best self and behavior;
- pervasive emotional detachments, perhaps a parent's emotional detachment from their child, perhaps children's detachment from other children in the family be they siblings or cousins;
- a parent making their child feel responsible for them by asking the child to behave like an adult caretaker;
- sexual inappropriateness by a parent, sibling, or other member of the family including grandparents, aunts, uncles, cousins, and even "trusted" family friends;

Notes

- hearing things about not having been wanted, about having been a surprise whom a parent or other family members felt forced to care for or perhaps felt "stuck with";

- hearing that a parent is "done" with having children and being a parent;

- changes in residence (regardless of how many times) due to circumstances like a parent's job relocation, fire, eviction, or the aftermath of a divorce; and

- a parent who was predominantly angry, sad, detached, or who could become one of these very quickly and unexpectedly.

And there are other examples of baffling, traumatic unsettledness due to emotional turmoil and unnecessary hurt in one's early inner circle of relationships and experiences.

A child might have indeed experienced traumas such as war or beatings. However, for a child *anything* that doesn't match the physical, sexual, and emotional safety the child instinctively expects from a parent and family members—experiences of hurt, turmoil, humiliation, anything that doesn't match—is traumatic for a child.

For the child, the household they are in is the world to them. No bafflement in that world can be dismissed as non-impacting. In fact, each bafflement within that world has a powerful impact. There's no comparing with other households. Each child comes to understand themself, the world, and life itself from what they experience in their own household.

> *For the child, the household they are in is the world to them.*
> *No bafflement in that world can be dismissed as non-impacting.*
> *Each child comes to understand themself, the world, and life itself*
> *from what they experience in their own household.*

Children are innately wired to do whatever is necessary to navigate their world, to survive the baffling emotional pain, unsettledness, fear, perhaps even terror which they experience there. Remember: this is baffling pain, unsettledness, fear, and terror for a child, as experienced in the mind, in the heart, in the entire being of a child.

So, each child has an instinctive, unconscious ability to file, archive, or flash freeze these difficult experiences. For a child it's a terrifying, traumatic unsettledness that any

---

Notes

kind of pain or inappropriateness—physical, sexual, or emotional—could be caused by those in their closest relational orbit. It is so terrifying that children instinctively call into service their unconscious ability to store the pain instantaneously, in a nanosecond, to survive it.

Later in life we often don't remember specific happenings, but *feelings* from childhood will reappear. Any feeling later in life—one that doesn't make sense, that we don't understand, that we question where it's coming from—is some of the old, stored pain that was traumatic for the child we once were. That stored, traumatic pain has gone nowhere. It's as if each person has a file folder within their invisible inner processing system titled: "Deal with this and figure it out later."

> *Any feeling later in life—one that doesn't make sense, that we don't understand, that we question where it's coming from— is some of the old, stored pain that was traumatic for the child we once were. That stored, traumatic pain has gone nowhere.*

The *later* designation was attached to every experience filed, archived, or flash frozen through our nanosecond survival skills. And this was the right plan of action for us to have followed as children because children have absolutely no idea what to do with pain, hurt, and fear when it's caused by a parent, family member, or another trusted person. The bafflement is beyond words and, because it's beyond words, it often gets acted out rather than talked out, *out* being the operative word. But even then, it's not all out.

Anything *stored* implies it will be sorted through *later*. It's just that no one ever actually told us that everything stored through filing, archiving, or flash freezing would show up one day to be processed. No one told us we would be sorting through—across our lifetime—all that we stored within ourself during childhood.

Our system is really quite protective of us by letting things come up and out bit by bit because we have no precise idea about how many moments of hurt or bafflement— even nanoseconds of hurt or bafflement—we had to file, archive, or flash freeze when we were children. We might have stored a big, significant event, or it might have been the split-second look of disappointment or rage on a parent's face.

Notes

Within one thirty-minute dinner, there might have been five moments that we stored: something said to us, something said by a parent, something said by or to a sibling, or nothing said and yet conveyed, even shouted, through a glare or an attitude.

If there were five quick moments that we stored within ourself during a thirty-minute evening meal, it's highly likely there were another five quick moments that we stored during the other 15.5 hours of a waking day. If ten moments of hurt or bafflement—even tiny ones—were stored in one day, in one year we would have stored 3,650 moments. After ten years of life as a child, we'd have 36,000+ moments on file.

This is why our emotional system is very protective of us and lets the stored hurt and bafflement surface and come out across our entire lifetime.

> *Because we potentially have 36,000+ baffling moments from childhood on file, our system is very protective of us and lets the stored hurt and bafflement surface and come out across our lifetime.*

Remember: When stored emotions come out, they do so with the exact degree of pain with which they went into storage. Any emotion flash frozen is completely raw again when defrosted. Thank goodness there's no mass extraction that can take place for these stored moments, no delete key or thumb drive which can free us from them all in just one click. It would be too much for our system to handle.

How *later* shows up today is best explained by returning to the metaphors already mentioned to describe how a child puts away their bafflements of emotional pain, unsettledness, fear, and even terror in order to survive such experiences.

- Something can happen today that could have a metaphorical quarter-centimeter of similarity to an event or emotion *filed* in childhood, and the filed-away experience from back then rattles loose now. It's as if what was napping in its filed-away state wakes up and is alive again.

  Example. You hear a song that gave you special comfort when you were a sophomore in high school, and you are flooded immediately with thoughts, images, memories from that time in your life. You did nothing consciously to pull forward these stored memories.

Notes

- Something happening today can have a magnetic quality such that whatever was *archived* back then is pulled with quick force out of storage and is suddenly right there before us now, even if there had been no conscious awareness of this event and its associated emotions for a long time—if ever. Even without any conscious awareness of that early life event then or now—all of a sudden—here it is.

  Example. Be aware of what comes to mind for you and how quickly it comes to mind when you read these two numbers: 9 / 11. How quickly—and through no conscious effort to remember—did images of the Twin Towers in New York come alive for you?

- For anything *flash frozen* during childhood as the method to store it and defer its processing until later, remember that it was flash frozen because it was emotional pain that we didn't know how to process or navigate—because we were children. We didn't have to flash freeze good experiences because we didn't have to protect ourself from them.

Here is a detailed look at how anything once flash frozen gets processed today. Experiences once flash frozen within us defrost in two ways:

- from excessive emotional *heat*, a term often used to describe stressful emotions, for example, "Let's bring down the temperature of this situation," and

- from something emotionally gentler, for example, room temperature warmth defrosting something frozen as it sits on the kitchen counter.

We use the word *heat* if something happens today that's emotionally difficult or stressful. We use the word *warmth* when indicating something gentle and good. Both emotional heat and emotional warmth can trigger the thawing of whatever difficult emotion we once flash froze, very often flash thawing it.

It may seem odd that something warm or pleasant today can thaw and even flash thaw something difficult that had been frozen within us. However, whether there's a similarity today to a difficult childhood emotion (hurt/"heat") or something today that's opposite to childhood (happy/"warm" rather than sad), thawing occurs.

When the once flash-frozen event or emotion flash thaws, the experience of this can in an instant feel as if it's a current-day experience. What, in fact, is going on is this: someone is experiencing the rawness that was interrupted when the experience was

Notes

flash frozen in the first place. Any food bought months ago and frozen at that time becomes raw again when thawed.

Flash-frozen childhood emotions follow the exact same principle. As children we unconsciously made a millisecond decision, an instinctive choice, to flash freeze a feeling that didn't seem healthy for us at the time. When it flash thaws later in life, the feeling from childhood picks up right where it left off, and we feel it in all its rawness.

As with the disappointing quality of freezer-burnt food, such an old emotion—now out, thawed, and raw—can feel even worse today than it initially did, but that doesn't mean it wasn't terribly painful in and of itself at the time for the child we were. Remember: That's why we flash froze it.

Another way that unsettling childhood experiences once flash frozen in childhood can flash thaw today is like what we do when watching a TV show or movie.

When we step away for a moment (to answer the phone, take a pizza out of the oven, change a load of laundry), we might use the pause or freeze button on the remote. Upon returning to the show or movie being watched, when the pause/freeze button is released, from where does the show pick up? From the exact place at which the action had been frozen.

Early life emotions that we flash froze follow a similar principle. When the pause or freeze button is rattled loose today for whatever reasons, by whatever trigger of emotional heat or warmth, the once flash-frozen emotion picks up from exactly where that moment of our childhood reality had been frozen. We unconsciously froze that moment of childhood in a nanosecond. It was our only way to survive the bafflement of the sad, devaluing, and perhaps even terrifying unsettledness being experienced.

So, what's really being experienced in the present—in all its rawness—is the difficult-for-a-child event and/or emotion that had been unconsciously frozen in childhood. Whatever had been paused/frozen is released and picks up right from where it left off—without missing a beat.

Example 1. _When your manager at work yells at you—doesn't just give feedback—and displays anger or animated annoyance, you end up feeling like a little kid because a parent talked to you the same way at times—or maybe always._

Notes

Example 2. *You spend a lovely evening with friends. They were genuinely interested in you, in what you had to say, in what's going on in your life. Once you get home, however, you feel sad for what appears to be no reason at all. You just had a wonderful evening. Your sadness doesn't make sense. The warmth of the evening has defrosted a sadness long-stored within you about times when a parent, maybe a sibling, seemed detached from and not interested in what you were sharing with them. Present day warmth defrosted a hurt flash frozen long ago.*

These are the creative techniques we instinctively, instantaneously, unconsciously engaged during childhood to buy time, to temporarily free ourself from having to know, process, and manage situations which were just too confusing and therefore too scary to consciously deal with when we were experiencing them.

Remember: for a child, these moments were traumatic, truly traumatic. If the child was without an adult who could help them make sense out of such moments and understand them, the trauma is not processed and stays stored within until it flash thaws one day.

Because we instinctively knew there were experiences that we simply didn't know what to do with, we froze those experiences for processing at another time.

> **Because we instinctively knew there were experiences that we simply didn't know what to do with, we froze those experiences for processing at another time.**

This was not an irresponsible nor cowardly thing to do. In fact, it was a brilliantly smart and self-respecting choice, even though it was an unconscious one. Although children have the radar to know when something isn't right, no child has the skills just yet to figure it out and do something about it. Some examples of this dynamic include:

Example 1. *If we had two parents, perhaps they didn't like each other, as subtle as that might have been. Perhaps they were openly hostile with each other. If the captains of the ship are at war, what ease or calm is there for any passengers on their ship?*

Example 2. *Perhaps we had a parent who was sad. Every child wants nothing more than to do what they instinctively presume every child should be able to do, even when flat on*

Notes

their back in their crib: bring a joyful smile to a parent's face. How unsettling if one of my earliest experiences of being myself is one of missing the mark in this way, something that unconsciously feels like and is emotionally recorded as a failure, a feeling that can persist— even subtly—across our lifetime.

Example 3. There may have been a time when we experienced a child at school or in the neighborhood being aggressive (bullying, belittling, frightening) with us. However, we don't feel comfortable enough to tell a parent because we expect them to also belittle us through comments like, "Toughen up!" or "Grow up!" In this case the parent, too, is a bully to some degree. Yes, the child can indeed and should toughen up and grow up, but this will happen so much more smoothly and quickly if the child's initial feelings are understood, honored, and comforted by the parent.

This would not be a parent being soft. It would be a parent being respectful enough to bravely be with their child in the reality of that child's feelings. Once respected by a parent, every child regardless of age can do a much better job of navigating whatever it is they are facing—even disrespect on the playground.

Example 4. We may have had a parent who was incapacitated due to illness, or a substance use disorder, or who tried to take their own life. In each of these cases, we would have been filled with worry about whether our parent would get better. We were scared and helpless, and we could do nothing with such feelings at an early age other than store them.

What happens later in life to the feelings we stored earlier? The feelings stored (the content of the experience was unconsciously stored in the subconscious as well) want to be known as having happened to us. It's the way that each of us, for the unconscious purpose of personal integrity, is given the task over time—usually against our will—of reading all the pages of our own autobiography. It's as if our feelings want a witness and, in fact, are insisting upon it. Each of us is that witness, our own witness.

Even though we may think and hope that the feelings and content of the experiences we stored in childhood would stay stored there forever and never again see the light of day, these records of our life don't see it that way. Our stored childhood feelings and experiences complied with the initial, self-protective instinct that they be stored because there was nothing else we could have done with them. They were stamped with the word *later* simply by the nature of their being stored.

Notes

However, these feelings and experiences want to be known precisely because they are significant parts of our life. For example, an adult's stories of being *physically* alone in a desert or forest, lost in a heavy fog, or caught in a war zone may be recounted and shared later in life—and sometimes quite often. So, too, do the stories want to be told of when—as children—we were all alone in an *emotional* desert or forest, lost in a heavy and scary emotional fog, or caught in an emotional war zone. These stories always find their way into the light of finally being seen, known, felt, understood.

Time and energy are misused with wishing that this wasn't the way our life story unfolds and how our stored childhood experiences get sorted through and understood. The energy wishing this task could be avoided is better used for actively, bravely seeing, knowing, and understanding the impacts that our childhoods will forever have on us.

The examples noted in this essay may not in and of themselves appear to be so unsettling. Two things, however, make them such. First, it was *a child* navigating these experiences, not an adult, in what they knew as the world. Second, while there may have been highlighted moments of unsettledness, most of these examples reflect what was in the child's home atmosphere—"in the air"—at all times, an unsettledness that was there for the child 24/7 whether consciously or not. Because unsettledness for a child equals *not safe*, unsettledness for a child is traumatic.

> *Because unsettledness for a child equals not safe,*
> *unsettledness for a child is traumatic.*

It is both sad and amazing to realize all that a child unconsciously does to navigate their traumas of unsettledness, of not being safe, to create their strategy for surviving.

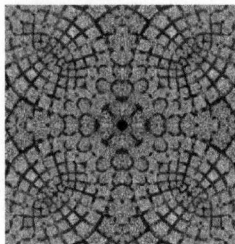

Notes

3. Struggle versus Challenge

Children have an unconscious, instinctive, instantaneous awareness for recognizing when experiences are such that they don't know what to do with them. This instinct causes children to store the experiences in a nanosecond because this is all they can do with situations and the accompanying emotions they don't know how to process or understand. When these experiences are so quickly stored through filing, archiving, or flash-freezing, a child is also unconsciously and quickly stamping them with the word *later*.

As children grow up, no one explains to them that they will instinctively store things they don't know how to navigate. No one explains that everything unconsciously stored and marked *later* during childhood would one day show up to be unpacked, sorted through, understood, and owned. So, how does *later* show up today, and in what form?

Struggle is the way by which *later* arrives. Every struggle—not challenge, but struggle—is the *showing up* of something from childhood about which we didn't know what to say or do at the time and therefore unconsciously filed, archived, or flash froze it—something that we marked *later*.

If we are willing to learn how to do so, managing struggle is the process by which we continue our recovery—across our lifetime—from the bafflements we experienced and stored when we were children: the bafflements of how we were regarded and treated as children, our confusion from any counterproductive messages we received from a parent and family members about ourself, about the world, about life.

> *Managing struggle is the process by which we continue our recovery—across our lifetime—from the bafflements we experienced and stored when we were children.*

The difference between a challenge and a struggle is this:

A challenge is something which engages a person. Something that's a challenge may puzzle and stump someone—for example, how to get something up or down a flight of

---

Notes

31

stairs—but engagement persists with the problem to be solved, with the situation to be figured out, with the opportunity to be experienced. A person might feel perplexed, but not trapped, not desperate. However, a struggle is when someone feels like they are going in circles, up against a wall, helpless, hopeless, desperate, blocked, trapped.

Every struggle today is revealing something of what life was like for us as children. Struggle is the costume by which an old, stored, baffling, childhood experience shows up today as fresh as when it first happened.

> *Struggle is the costume by which an old, stored, baffling, childhood experience shows up today as fresh as when it first happened.*

It's as if something stored within us from childhood unconsciously connects to a situation today that may not be circumstantially the same, but it *feels like* something we experienced and stored as a child. The heat or warmth of a current situation defrosts the frozen childhood moment, and the thawed feeling jumps out and piggybacks on something today. The current situation becomes transportation for the stored experience. The difficult, stored experiences of childhood will do what children do: take a piggyback ride whenever one can be had.

A common saying when we're struggling, when we don't know what to do or what to say, is the statement, "I feel beside myself." The phrase *beside myself* is truer and more accurate than we've ever realized. It means that we're feeling:

- beside the self I once was as a child, and
- beside words and moments that we filed, archived, or flash froze in lightning speed in childhood.

Yes, *beside myself*—beside the self I once was—is being beside the moments in my life that I once froze in suspended animation in a nanosecond, feelings as alive now as they were when my instinctive ability to store them in childhood was unconsciously engaged. So, whenever we are struggling, there is a current component at play for sure. But first and foremost, we are feeling *beside myself,* beside my past self, feeling like the child I once was—LTCIOW.

Notes

> *Whenever we are struggling,*
> *there is a current component at play for sure.*
> *But first and foremost, we are feeling beside myself,*
> *beside my past self, feeling like the child I once was—LTCIOW.*

<u>*Example*</u>. *Someone's life partner uncharacteristically "blew up" over something without any apparent reason for doing so. Something from their partner's childhood just flash thawed. The person on the receiving end of this is in shock, feels paralyzed, is struggling, feels beside themself not knowing what to do.*

Experiencing this blow-up has unconsciously flooded the receiving partner with their own frozen—now flash-thawed—childhood experience of when their usually kind and peaceful parent would suddenly get enraged for whatever reason. When that happened, it was a traumatic experience for the child they once were—one of shock, of course, and then one of terror: "Who did my parent just become? When will be the next time my parent changes so quickly? This makes no sense. What am I supposed to do with this shock and fear about my parent (or whomever in the family)?"

So, a struggle is the indication that someone is beside themself, caught experiencing two very real moments in time: one today—be it a moment of heat (negative) or warmth (positive)—and one that's a baffling, painful moment frozen in childhood and delayed for processing until now.

> *A struggle is the indication that someone is beside themself,*
> *caught experiencing two very real moments in time:*
> *one today, and one frozen in childhood*
> *and delayed for processing until now.*

That's why when we're struggling, we feel a heightened level of frustration. Without consciously thinking about it in this way, we are trapped between our life today and our life as a child, living in two realities simultaneously—living today and also living beside a now-thawed, painful bafflement of the self we once were as a child.

This dynamic is active in non-childhood-related examples, too.

Notes

Example 1. When you see a photo of someone who is no longer your friend, and all over again you feel the emotions connected with this person and the end of that friendship.

Example 2. Any discussion or news report about the insurrection at the U.S. Capitol on January 6, 2021, can become an experience of feeling "beside the self I once was" as you remember originally witnessing or first learning about the events of that day.

This is how we can feel beside ourself so quickly.

The same is true for everything—*everything*—we flash froze when we were children. A certain scent can instantaneously remind us of either the body odor or the cologne of someone who physically assaulted us with their belt or shoe when we were a child. Mornings can routinely be unsettling for us because they are visceral reminders of how each morning as a child was characterized by not knowing what that day would bring by way of encounters with a parent or other family member.

The feelings of our painful, early life, our original experiences of being ourself, of living our life at that time, can, as one client put it, "shoot back like fireworks."

By fine-tuning our *emotional reflexes* over time, with practice we can become increasingly limber at catching each intruding, hijacking, early life story—any experience that was long ago marked *later* and that shows up in the *now*. We then would use our *emotional muscle*—something being strengthened over time—to hold the story, look at it, take it apart, feel it, understand it, name it, perhaps catch our breath from it, and by taking the time to do so, diffuse it. Proficiency in these skills will come with diligent practice.

There may still be something current to navigate afterward, but we have just shifted from being in a place of struggle, caught between two very real moments of life, to being in a place of challenge where we have agency and are not feeling paralyzed, held hostage, trapped, or desperate, where we're not feeling *beside myself* any longer.

Every feeling is real, but not every feeling experienced is about now. *Beside myself* feelings, struggle feelings, are feelings rattled loose by something in the now from our internal childhood emotional freezer, from our collection of paused early life moments.

> *Every feeling is real, but not every feeling experienced is about now.*

Notes

Because of this, it's critical to learn and continually put into practice distinguishing the collision of something that's a part of *now* and something that was a part of *back then*, to look at the two components of this simultaneous reality in chronological order. We may not be able to do so right at that moment, but whenever we can, it won't take much time to do.

Each time we use our emotional reflexes to catch what's going on—an old, old story having just defrosted which is piggybacking on the now—and as we rely on our emotional muscles to hold it and sort through it, we move from struggle to challenge. We set down the intruding early life reality and, in so doing, regain footing for navigating today's challenge effectively.

Just like feeling *beside myself* is a proof that we are feeling something very old from our childhood emotional freezers, another proof that we are feeling something old is when we are using either the word *so* or the word *too*, words of overreaction or excessive reaction:

- I'm so angry, scared, hurt, upset, overwhelmed (emotional heat).
- I'm so elated, happy, relieved (emotional warmth).
- This is too much.
- I'm so impacted by this.
- It's just too scary for me.

It is truly possible for us to effectively navigate through any collision between the feelings of today's experiences and the defrosted, intruding, raw feelings of our early life stories. These old, intruding feelings can't be quieted by anyone other than ourself. A parent lost their chance long ago. Not even a significant other can do so today.

Medication may provide some respite from these feelings by numbing them, putting them into a gentle coma, or by giving someone a leap-frog boost over them. However, whether the feelings are numbed and temporarily put to sleep, or whether they're overridden, the feelings go nowhere. They will attach themselves at some point to whatever opportunity may present itself, their determined way to escape from someone's childhood emotional freezer.

Notes

The dynamic of struggle is managed when we catch, hold, and sort through the colliding feelings. By doing so, we come to know and own the truth of our early life more and more: the story of what we had to navigate and survive as a child, and the awareness of its impact on us.

Relief from being trapped beside myself, beside the self we once were as a child, then arrives all on its own—and naturally so.

> *Relief from being trapped beside myself,*
> *beside the self we once were as a child,*
> *then arrives all on its own—and naturally so.*

<u>Example</u>. Consider a spouse facing the fact that their partner has been having an inappropriate emotional or sexual affair. Will this rock the hurting spouse to their core? Absolutely it will. Will it take time to learn, listen, check for genuine remorse on the part of the offender, catch one's breath, and determine whether one can move forward in life with this person or not? Absolutely.

However, when no perspective seems to come about for the offended person, when the person flooded with hurt blocks every plan for navigating this situation, when the devastated person seems stuck in their hurt, this is evidence that the heavy challenge of this terribly difficult situation is also a debilitating struggle for the offended person. Childhood pain is being defrosted and experienced in addition to the awful current hurt, insult, and betrayal.

The emotional heat of the current heartbreak has unearthed, rattled loose, defrosted, something from the offended spouse's childhood freezer which, during their childhood, was a great betrayal of trust. Remembering that every experience has two parts—the content of the experience and what it felt like—perhaps the offended person once sensed or actually learned that a parent was having either an emotional or physical affair with someone. Perhaps their parent made fun of them in front of other family members or friends. Perhaps the offended person's parent promised to be at a sports event but never showed up.

Any betrayal of what we expect someone to be is indeed painful, sometimes painful beyond words. When there's a double hit of such pain—the heated current betrayal of what we expect someone to be <u>and</u> a defrosted betrayal from childhood of what we expected a parent

Notes

36

or family member to be (regardless of the degree of the betrayal in childhood, because any betrayal for a child is traumatic)—it's critical that it be recognized for what it is. This recognition is how effective agency can return to the offended person today, how peace has any chance of returning at all.

Is this understanding and perspective intended to shift the problem behavior from the offender to the offended? Absolutely not. However, if the offended person is blocked or stuck, they must unpack both the pain of the current situation and the unearthed pain from their inner place of early life hurt, or they will not regain their footing. They will not be fair to themself, nor will they have their best decision-making skills at hand for either reconciling with their partner or for moving forward separately.

Another way to understand struggle is by using the concept of an emotional tornado. In brief, a tornado is the convergence of warm air meeting cool air that causes a rotating wall of cloud to form. The collision of these two fronts catches up into itself everything in its path, taking it all hostage into a ferocious swirl. This is true of our emotional self, too.

If the colliding emotional forces are something warm (good) meeting something in cold storage within us, or something heated/hot (difficult) happening today that flash thaws something that had been in rock-solid frozen storage within us from long ago— from childhood—the contrasts of warmth or heat and cold, of now and long ago, are fueling a collision that is a powerfully assaulting, distressing experience within an individual or between two people.

Example 1. A hot front—the heat of the emotionally disappointing situation of not being included in a gathering of friends—flash thaws something that had been in our childhood emotional freezer, perhaps a time when we so wanted siblings, cousins, or friends to include us in something, but they didn't. The current emotionally distressing moment has flash thawed childhood pain—a pain that is now as raw and alive as when it was flash frozen. We're now swirling and churning, "beside myself" in this tornado of colliding new and old distress. In this example, current emotional heat defrosted frozen childhood pain that was <u>similar</u> *to today's pain.*

Example 2. A warm front—the warmth of something very good like being at ease with certain friends—flash thaws feelings from when we didn't feel at ease with a parent or with other members of our family, something we expected would not only be possible but would be there naturally. We're unconsciously swept into the swirl of today's good experience

Notes

37

colliding with the defrosted childhood distress and then feel "beside myself" with distress today. In this example, a current moment of warmth flash thawed a distressing childhood experience that was the <u>opposite</u> of today's good experience.

Whenever we are struggling, there's an emotional tornado swirling: something going on today—emotionally difficult (heat) or emotionally positive (warmth)—and something simultaneously flash thawing from our childhood emotional freezer. To diffuse the tornado:

1. Acknowledge that something from the childhood freezer has just thawed—even if we don't know specifically just yet what's defrosted.

2. If possible, right then—or for sure later—identify the specific intruding childhood component of the struggle, feeling it for what it is: a frozen experience and emotion from long ago.

> *To diffuse the emotional tornado,*
> *identify and feel the intruding childhood component for what it is:*
> *a frozen experience and emotion from long ago.*

It's only by first acknowledging that an old, childhood component is at play—and specifically identifying it as soon as possible—that we can diffuse an emotional tornado and find our footing to either navigate and resolve the heated issue at hand or return to enjoying the goodness of a warm moment.

So, whether it's being beside myself or caught up in an emotional tornado within—or between us and someone else—the conscious recognition that we are struggling will start the process that shifts us from being the prisoner of a struggle to having agency with a challenge. We manage the struggle through our awareness by connecting the dots back to childhood. This is the process by which—across our lifetime—we continue our recovery from the painful bafflements we experienced and stored when we were children, including:

- bafflements of how we were regarded and treated as children;
- confusion from any counterproductive messages we received from a parent

Notes

and family members about ourself, about the world, about life itself;

- childhood hurts that show up today in those moments when we feel "beside myself";

- stored, painful emotions that defrost from our childhood freezer; and

- early life stories that show up in the emotional tornado of something heated or warm today meeting something once long ago frozen-in-time within us.

Notes

4. As Basic as One, Two, Three

In our earliest years of life, diapers collected the physical waste from our bodies. As we are taught and then encouraged to manage the elimination of physical wastes and toxins, the processes were often called going *Number 1* (to release liquid waste and toxins) and going *Number 2* (to eliminate solid waste and toxins).

We were even rewarded for doing each of these functions better and better—eventually successfully and independently—and without much thought or difficulty. We had accidents, of course, as we began learning and mastering each process, but we eventually learned how to do both. Both became a natural part of everyday life.

However, very few of us were ever taught how to release emotional waste and toxins. We weren't taught how to go (what we'll refer to here as) *Number 3* effectively—if at all. In fact, most people were told to not go Number 3, to not release their emotional waste and toxins. Instead, most children were told things like:

- "Don't say things like that."

- "That's not true."

- "Don't talk that way about [whatever or whomever]."

- "Who do you think you are saying something like that?"

- "Don't think that way."

- "You don't know what you're talking about."

To avoid the punishment of humiliating words, attitudes, and/or being deprived of something (for example, no supper, being grounded, being sent to our rooms, being deprived of the kindness or approval of a parent) that would often follow, we complied. We seldom and perhaps never took the chance to release our emotional waste and toxins in childhood or since in an aware and responsible way.

Some people release their emotional waste and toxins during their lives by being hard in various ways on others. Some of us do this release by being hard on ourself.

Notes

However, to some degree, all of us have parked some and perhaps the majority of our emotional waste and toxins—especially from childhood—in the nearest place we could store, file, flash freeze it all: within ourself.

The emotional waste and toxins that we kept inside ourself from those earliest days and years of our lives never went anywhere. And so, along the way, the waste and toxins release themselves—they defrost—whenever there's a moment of emotional heat (difficulty), emotional warmth (goodness), and also when we're especially weary physically, mentally, and/or emotionally, a tiredness which could feel like either heat (exhausted) or warmth (pleasantly quiet).

We unconsciously release on others—and sometimes on ourself—the emotional waste and toxins we were told to keep to ourself, told to swallow, which we unconsciously flash froze. We complied *with not going* Number 3 just as we complied *with going* Numbers 1 and 2.

A client in their early thirties, after hearing about Numbers 1, 2, and 3 said, "So, Number 1 is pee. Number 2 is poop. But Number 3 is s##t." Exactly.

> *A client in their early thirties, after hearing*
> *about Numbers 1, 2, and 3 said,*
> **"So, Number 1 is pee. Number 2 is poop. But Number 3 is s##t."**

That's...

- why we have either said to someone or had it said to us, "Don't dump your s##t on me."
- what it really means when we say, "I'm feeling really s##tty right now."
- why we say that someone is "full of s##t" because of their behaviors, attitudes, or beliefs.

Each time we've said any of this we've been right. We just didn't know right about what, or how right we were in what we were saying.

Notes

It is a responsibility for every person to learn the sensations within us that indicate when our emotional system is about to go Number 3, just as early in life we learned to recognize the signals when our body was telling us it was time to go Numbers 1 and 2. Saying "Nature's calling" came to be a polite way for us to say that we had to go Numbers 1 and 2. The call of nature that it's time to go Number 3—perhaps that we are already going or have already gone Number 3—is when we feel ourself *struggling*.

Struggling is our emotional system's "nature's calling" indicator that some of the old, stored, hurtful, baffling feelings from childhood are being released from frozen storage. As we learn to recognize this emotional sensation of struggling, we will more and more avoid s##tting on anyone else—or on ourself.

We'll have accidents, just as we did when learning to go Numbers 1 and 2. Those early life accidents had to be cleaned up, usually by an adult or someone older than us in the house. However, when an accident of Number 3 happens today, we have to do the clean-up ourself.

When we become aware that we just went Number 3, or when we sense we are about to do so, it's important to clean up our Number 3 just as we clean up Numbers 1 and 2: with paper. Putting pen-to-paper—not fingers to keyboard—is the way we relocate our emotional waste and toxins rather than dumping them on ourself or on anyone else. Even if at the time it would be easier to enter our emerging Number 3 feelings into our phones, transferring them to paper at some point is important.

Pen-to-paper is important because something physiological will be giving aid to something emotional. Our dominant arm acts as the off ramp for the defrosted feelings within us. Writing or printing pulls out clogged up, traffic-jammed thoughts and thawed feelings, and our hand transfers them to, parks them on, a piece of paper.

These puzzle pieces of our struggling literally land someplace where we can hold them rather than them holding us. We can see them and separate what's going on today from whatever has defrosted from our childhood emotional freezer.

We can then put the new puzzle pieces of our childhood story together and know them, feel them, for what they are—which is the best way to diffuse and quiet them.

Notes

Even if we have an accident and go Number 3 before we can catch what's coming out, writing about it afterward cleans it up. Paper absorbs emotional waste just as paper absorbs Number 1 and Number 2 waste. Cleaning up Number 3 in this way is what can simply be called *writing*, dumping the inner emotional noise, dumping stored and now loosened-up emotional waste and toxins. This is not quite the same as journaling.

> *Cleaning up #3 is what can simply be called <u>writing</u>, dumping the inner emotional noise, dumping stored and now loosened up emotional waste and toxins. This is not quite the same as journaling.*

Journaling is indeed a way to record our thoughts and feelings, generally reflective writing stereotypically done within a linen-covered or leather-bound book, on a finer grade of paper, and often with one or more ribbons as page markers. Journaling is often writing that we want to keep. However, journaling's focus is not *primarily* to get out emotional waste and toxins.

We may or may not want to keep all our Number 3 writing. If something especially powerful or helpful comes from within while we're doing our Number 3 writing, some of these highlights can be transferred and kept within a journal. However, going Number 3 as it's being described here calls for utilitarian paper, something like a legal pad or a spiral notebook.

The more we write, the more emotional waste and toxins come out. Such writing really becomes insight into our lives. It can bring us some relief because of the better understanding of ourself and our inner dynamics that results.

Even the struggling we may do when trying to fall asleep is our emotional system's way of nudging us to get something out. We never think twice about going Number 1 once before bedtime. Maybe our system would benefit from us going Number 3—and writing, if even for just five or ten minutes—before bedtime, too.

The same principle applies if we wake up during the night and can't sleep. If we naturally get up and go Number 1 during the night when our physical system alerts us to do so, it's important to get up and go Number 3 if our emotional system is alerting us to do so, when our mind is going in circles and we can't quiet it down. Even if we get up

---

Notes

and write for as long as thirty minutes or more, it's likely that we will then be able to go back to bed and get some good sleep.

Engaging in such an experience of writing can even feel meditative. In fact, writing may be the best form of meditation because its aim is not only to bring some quiet to inner noise, but also to get some of the inner noise *out*. Meditation quiets noise inside, but it doesn't facilitate getting it out. Writing does both.

> *Writing may be the best form of meditation because its aim is not only to bring some quiet to inner noise, but also to get some of the inner noise <u>out</u>. Meditation quiets noise inside, but it doesn't facilitate getting it out. Writing does both.*

Writing lets us hold *it*, whatever may be holding us inside, rather than *it* continuing to hold us. By doing our writing, getting some of the inner noise out, meditation can then be less difficult to engage with, and it can more easily provide its own wonderful benefits.

As we go Number 3, we make new room within for our own natural thoughts and feelings to flow, thoughts and feelings that have been blocked by old, traffic-jammed but now-thawed, emotional waste and poison inside. The relief is similar to the relief experienced after tensely waiting to go Number 1 or Number 2 and not knowing if you'd arrive at the bathroom in time to do so.

Just as we've learned to manage going Numbers 1 and 2, it's critically important for each of us to learn how to manage our going Number 3. What makes this more difficult is that we are not only trying to manage the Number 3s of today, we are also cleaning out the Number 3s that never flowed out from us across the years of our life from the time we were children. In fact, we did the most storing of our Number 3s when we were little because it was implied that we shouldn't go Number 3, and so we complied.

When we are struggling emotionally—whatever it might be about—there are two steps involved with the writing process for going Number 3:

1. Write down whatever is making the noise inside. You may be upset. You may feel shut down. You may not exactly know what to write. Write about that. Just start writing and writing. Your writing might even look like scribble at first or like an

Notes

45

agitated slashing of the pen on the paper. Even this is putting on paper feelings for which you haven't yet found the words. Don't be concerned about what you write or how you phrase things or what spelling or punctuation you use. You may get a lot out in five or ten minutes. Once you write a small amount, a flow may continue and more might come forth. You may find yourself writing for thirty minutes or more.

2. After you conclude your writing, slowly read it and spotlight in some way—circling, underlining, highlighting—any words or phrases that jump out at you as having punch or importance. What you will find is that you could have said or written these highlighted words and phrases when you were eighteen years old or younger, most especially when you were still of a single-digit age.

In doing this second step, you will literally see what has defrosted, how something today has thawed out feelings within you that were unconsciously flash frozen years ago. These defrosted, early life emotions became mixed together with whatever is going on present day within you. This is the *beside myself struggle* or *emotional tornado* in which you have found yourself.

You will have captured two sets of puzzle pieces: how you describe the *noise* within you—what you're feeling now—plus words that reveal what you were feeling *as a child*. By separating back then from now, you will catch your breath, realize something additional about your early life journey, and regain your agency and footing for whatever you are facing today.

Here's an example of writing. Read the person's original writing first, then read the reprint with the punchy, emotion-filled words highlighted in gray. The original writing...

I'm struggling with something very familiar.

In the past when I've faced administrative tasks that require me to do detailed, accurate mathematical work where I've had to create or find support for the numbers, I panic. I know this feeling well from the past and it causes me to be obsessive and fearful, and to want to run away.

This has come up because I'm facing completing the PPP (Payroll Protection Plan during the 2020 pandemic) forgiveness application. Not only am I unsure of what to do, it feels like I don't have the documentation that's necessary. Clearly, I got the loan, so what I

Notes

submitted must have been accepted, but I am circling around submitting the forgiveness application because I don't feel I am doing it right, don't feel I deserve it, am afraid I don't understand it and/or will make a mistake. I have asked about simply paying it off (I don't need the funds) and am unsure as to why I even applied in the first place.

Part of me wants to take the easy way out and pay it off. The other part says, no, you need to figure out how to do this, and even if they don't forgive it, you can pay it off then.

The struggle—trying to choose between allowing myself to risk making a mistake and being scared by that versus feeling guilty about wanting to walk away from this task and being scared by that—is miserable. Either way, I suffer.

For sure I want this behind me as it is taking up too much head space and creating anxiety that takes me back to prior times. Ugh. It is going to be dealt with one way or the other— and very soon.

And now the original writing reviewed and highlighted...

I'm struggling with something very familiar.

In the past when I've faced administrative tasks that require me to do detailed, accurate mathematical work where I've had to create or find support for the numbers, I panic. I know this feeling well from the past and it causes me to be obsessive and fearful, and to want to run away.

This has come up because I'm facing completing the PPP (Payroll Protection Plan during the 2020 pandemic) forgiveness application. Not only am I unsure of what to do, it feels like I don't have the documentation that's necessary. Clearly, I got the loan, so what I submitted must have been accepted, but I am circling around submitting the forgiveness application because I don't feel I am doing it right, don't feel I deserve it, am afraid I don't understand it and/or will make a mistake. I have asked about simply paying it off (I don't need the funds) and am unsure as to why I even applied in the first place.

Part of me wants to take the easy way out and pay it off. The other part says, no, you need to figure out how to do this, and even if they don't forgive it, you can pay it off then.

Notes

The struggle—trying to choose between allowing myself to risk making a mistake and being scared by that possibility versus feeling guilty about wanting to walk away from this task and being scared by that—is miserable. Either way, I suffer.

For sure I want this behind me as it is taking up too much head space and creating anxiety that takes me back to prior times. Ugh. It is going to be dealt with one way or the other—and very soon.

The heaviness of this person's struggle was the collision of something currently going on (a situation of emotional heat) with the defrosted old feelings of doing math homework in fourth grade, sitting at the kitchen table with their parent, the parent's observations and comments adding great stress to the child. Highlighted phrases extracted from this writing sample that illustrate this include:

- "tasks that require me to do detailed, accurate mathematical work,"

- "I panic,"

- "I know this feeling well from the past and it causes me to be obsessive, fearful, and want to run away,"

- "I am circling around,"

- "I don't feel I am doing it right, don't feel I deserve it, am afraid I don't understand it and/or will make a mistake,"

- "You need to figure out how to do this,"

- "The struggle—allowing myself to risk making a mistake and being scared by that versus feeling guilty about wanting to walk away from this task and being scared by that—is miserable,"

- "Either way, I suffer,"

- "I want this behind me," and

- "creating anxiety" [being afraid].

Going back to read whatever was originally written and doing some highlighting will illustrate how situations today can flash thaw feelings and experiences we once had to flash freeze as children in order to survive them. In the reading and highlighting, the

Notes

two colliding realities are separated from each other, and footing returns to navigate the issue at hand today. For example, here's one of the highlighted lines from the writing sample on the previous pages with some added words of perspective that could follow the "dumping" of this inner noise:

"I know this feeling well from the past and it causes me to be obsessive and fearful, and to want to run away."

Let me catch my breath from being flooded with the "obsessive and fearful, and to want to run away" feelings from childhood. Let me catch my breath, realize I had to navigate these as a child, and be amazed at how hard I was working as a child to do so. Let me catch my breath again. My footing is returning. The spinning is quieting. I'm no longer feeling so beside myself.

It can be especially helpful to keep a log of any highlighted sections within our writing. Doing so will offer focus for referencing back, for further reflection, and for a phrase bank of our own individual awareness phrases. In this case, *obsessive and fearful, and to want to run away,* are old, toxic feelings we had to navigate in childhood and are not about today. That's a phrase worth keeping and remembering.

It's so important to recognize our inner noise, our *struggling,* for what it is: emotional waste and toxins from our childhood. Very simply, it's time for us to take going Number 3 as seriously as we take going Numbers 1 and 2.

> *Very simply, it's time for us to take going Number 3*
> *as seriously as we take going Numbers 1 and 2.*

Going Numbers 1 and 2 can be annoying at times, but we haven't looked for medical help or a prescription to completely free us from having to do either of these elimination functions. It will be a great fairness to ourself if we incorporate going Number 3—with whatever regularity—into the natural flow of our life, too.

***

5. Unpacking and Weeding

Unpacking

Early life experiences that were baffling, unsettling, and therefore traumatic for the children we once were have been unconsciously stored in an emotional freezer within us. Something happens in life today that—through nothing we deliberately do or don't do—flash thaws one of these early life stories and delivers them to the door of our consciousness. It's how these early life stories find their way into the light of our knowing, seeing, feeling, and understanding them.

Because each early life story contains both content details and recorded feelings, there's a lot of noise associated with the arrival of one of these stories. The noise is at first experienced as something overwhelming, perhaps an overwhelming anxiety, stress, anger, or self-hate, something which seems to take us over. Its grip on us is so great, so raw, that we think the feeling is about today, something out of control, something wrong with us.

However, the noise is really about the historical record of our childhood. Even though we may trace it to something in life along the way, such as a previous romantic relationship, it can be traced even further back to life experiences when we were eighteen years old or younger, even back to when we were in single-digit ages, and sometimes all the way back to our time in the crib and even in the womb.

Once we trace back to our life in single-digit ages, we can begin to realize the impact of a parent who was there or not there, and how they were there or not there. That's why our filed-away stories that get rattled loose from storage and land at the doorstep of our consciousness can be called UPS deliveries: Unwanted Parental Surprises.

Just like the UPS delivery person who rings the doorbell and quickly returns to their truck, so do our stored, early life stories deliver themselves, ask us to pick them up, and invite us to look through them. As we do so, we will experience feelings, remember details—sometimes experience the feelings without the details, sometimes remember details before experiencing the feelings—but it's all from our collection of frozen childhood stories and emotions for which *later*, the time to process them, has arrived.

When one of these early life stories arrives at our doorstep, we do with it what we'd do with any UPS delivery: we unpack it. Have any of us ever not unpacked a UPS delivery?

Notes

If we're unpacking a box that's not newly delivered, but one discovered by surprise in the basement, attic, garage, or storage locker, we often don't remember everything that we stored there until we open it and sort through it. Some of what we find may rattle us, but after going through things, we'll likely feel the satisfaction that comes from unpacking and sorting through something, and we'll feel lighter for having done so.

The key here is to realize that the overwhelming experience with which we are struggling today is, in fact, a set of feelings and details that we had once nanosecond-stored when we were children. The word *overwhelming* is important. Something today draws forth or rattles loose something that had been in storage within us, and what was in storage then sits on top of the current-day situation, experience, or feeling—overwhelming it, overwhelming us.

The overwhelming nature of a rush of *anger* we may be feeling is old, flash-frozen anger from a time we once (or often) felt hurt and powerless as a child—a childhood experience over which we had no influence or power to make otherwise at the time—which has now defrosted and sits on top of a current-day anger. It's now freed from storage and on top of or mixed in with the current-day situation.

Example. When someone accuses us of something we didn't do, we feel overwhelmed with anger. A situation today has unconsciously brought up the feelings from when a parent did the same—accused us of something we didn't do—and we had no resource available within us at that time to address the hurt and anger we were feeling. Both the hurt and anger had to be flash frozen.

The overwhelming part of a current-day *fear* is an old fear once frozen in time that's now thawed and raw again, as raw as when we first stored it, sitting on top of a fear today.

Example. We may be excessively worried about someone going to a party where alcohol will be plentiful even though this person is very responsible regarding their alcohol use. What has unconsciously been brought forward and is overwhelming us are the memories of times when a parent would come home drunk. They were times of a double fear: fear for the parent traveling to get home after drinking, and the fear of what might happen at home once the parent arrived. This double fear had to be flash frozen because, as a child, we could do nothing else with it.

Notes

Overwhelming *self-hate* is the defrosted record of when, as children, we unconsciously directed toward ourself, parked on ourself, any number of moments of hate:

- the hate we had for what a parent or family member may have been doing to us or someone else,

- the hate we had for ourself as a child because of something we couldn't influence or change,

- when we hated a certain situation, and

- when we hated feeling hate at all.

Example 1. *The situation of a parent or family member accusing us of something that we didn't do was already referenced when addressing overwhelming anger. This parent or family member was likely deflecting responsibility onto us for something they weren't doing right in our regard. We hated that they were doing this to us, and we hated the fact that we were hating something about them. We parked this hate on ourself and began believing it was a character defect in us, rather than owning the hate as something we had valid reason to feel regarding this hurtful situation.*

Example 2. *We so wished we could make something better and happier for a parent but couldn't even bring a smile to their face or some respite for their sadness. We hated ourself for not being able to lighten our parent's load, for being such a failure as their child.*

Example 3. *We were aware—consciously or not—that those closest to us had no genuine interest in us, found no value in having us in their lives or in knowing us. What a failure for the child we were if those closest to us had no interest in us. Allowing ourself to hate this reality frightened us because we thought it could lead us to hate them, and we didn't want to hate them. And we hated the fact that we were even put in a position of hate for those who regarded and treated us in this way. So, we parked this hate on ourself, started to hate ourself instead, and began thinking of ourself as hateful.*

And remember: we'll often hear ourself using the words *so* and *too* to describe something overwhelming that we're experiencing, sure signs—indicators—that we're struggling, that something has defrosted from our childhood emotional freezer.

Notes

The concept of unpacking applies to all of our childhood emotional storage places: internal, subconscious, file cabinets, archives, and freezers. Once unpacked, sorted through, cleaned out—to whatever degree but at least a bit more for now—we feel some accomplishment, some relief, and even some degree of freedom. This becomes as literal emotionally as what we've each experienced settling into a new residence. The more we unpack:

- the more we feel moved in,

- the more room there is for us to move around, and

- the more room there is for the right people and the right experiences to come in and join us.

> *The more we unpack, the more we feel moved in, the more room there is for us to move around, and the more room there is for the right people and the right experiences to come in and join us.*

This is the dividend we reap when we unpack what's stored within us. The unpacking process continues throughout our lifetime as the boxes, archives, or freezer empty their contents and invite us to sort through them, unpack them, and know them as experiences that happened to us.

Weeding

Because there is uniqueness, beauty, and goodness found in each of our personalities, styles, wants, and interests, it's appropriate to look at each of our individual selves as a garden.

In every garden in the world, no matter how beautiful it may be, how well-supported with monetary investment, how well-tended by dedicated, experienced professionals or volunteers—be they beautiful gardens in Japan, the national botanic gardens of Africa, the gardens at the Vatican, Buckingham Palace or the White House, the magnificent gardens in Buenos Aires, or your grandparent's garden—there are weeds that crop up.

Notes

Every gardener will tell us:

- "I fertilize a few times a year."

- "I water when nature isn't providing enough."

- "What I have to stay on top of are the weeds."

Consider all the phrases we use to describe weeds in a garden:

- "They keep cropping up."

- "They're overtaking everything."

- "They're so thick that I'm tripping over them."

So, another way to look at what may lie dormant within us is to consider the painful old feelings and details stored there like weeds which got seeded early in life in the garden of who we each are. Weeds can lie dormant for a long time, and then they can crop up. The painful bafflements we had to experience as children are like weeds planted in early life by a parent and family members.

All that's in our childhood emotional freezer—experiences and feelings we didn't know how to process because we were children—*we* unconsciously put there. However, our *parents and family members* were the ones who consciously or unconsciously—it doesn't matter—planted *weeds of false beliefs and false presumptions* about who we are, about life, about what we deserve in life, about what we should expect in life. They did this by how they regarded and treated us.

> *All that's in our childhood emotional freezer we unconsciously put there.*
> *However, our parents and family members were the ones who planted*
> *weeds of false beliefs and false presumptions about who we are,*
> *about life, about what we deserve in life,*
> *about what we should expect in life.*

How a child is regarded and treated by a parent and their family members becomes the self-definition for that child. Until this sense of self is looked at with an understanding

---

Notes

of its origins, the unexamined sense of self will continue to define how we think, feel, act, and live each day.

Both the positive impacts and the weeds planted by a parent and family members are the most *impactful* of all experiences in our lifetime, and they come with a lifetime warranty. The good will continue serving us well. The weeds will crop up again and again—because that's what weeds do.

A parent and family members will most likely not remain the most important people in our life. Life partners, our children, and good friends become the most important. However, a parent and family members will forever be the most *impactful* because our experiences of how they regarded and treated us are the first experiences we have of life, of the world, of other people, and of ourself.

A child may be given the blatant or even subtle message that because of their birth, because of their existence, a parent:

- didn't have as much time for things they wanted to do in life as they had before the child's birth,

- had to leave a job they loved and so lost a sense of their professional self, or

- was forced to share a spotlight which previously had often been exclusively shining on the parent.

This child will then forever have one or more of these weeds of "shame on me [the child]" cropping up within them, overwhelming them, choking them out, tripping them up across their lifetime. They might then:

- believe they are a bad person because they took away from a parent's life, did damage to a parent's life, rather than bring joy to their parent;

- feel of little interest or like a nobody if the parent's life was more interesting prior to their child's existence; or

- feel like a fraud or imposter because the child presents themself as a good and happy person but at core feels otherwise, that is, believes they are a bad person and feels so very sad.

Notes

No child can develop an initial self-concept, sense of self, other than what they see in their parent's eyes and on their parent's face, what is heard in their parent's voice, what is felt in their parent's touch and embrace. If these are pleasant and safe experiences, the child develops a positive sense of self and a sense of at-homeness with themself.

If these are not pleasant and safe experiences, if they are experiences of detachment, annoyance, or displeasure, then the garden of who this child is becomes filled with unsettledness and self-doubt. Such weeds will keep cropping up across a person's lifetime.

The emotional bafflements we experienced because of our parents and family members are deeply rooted in us. They became the truest source of the phrase *first impressions are lasting* because these impacts are both first and forever. Sorting through them and making sense of them takes a lifetime.

This is so true of early life bafflements, but also of anything in life that simply should not have happened—events such as the horrors of the U.S. Civil War, the massacres of students at Margery Stoneman Douglas High School in Florida and at Robb Elementary in Texas, shoppers gunned down at the Tops Friendly Market in New York State—among so many other sad, sad events.

Experiences that cause a child to not feel safe, to not be able to trust, to not feel connected to themself or their caregivers, simply should not have happened and are traumatic.

> *Experiences that cause a child to not feel safe,*
> *to not be able to trust,*
> *to not feel connected to themself or their caregivers,*
> *simply should not have happened and are traumatic.*

Sometimes weeds can add to a landscape. Queen Anne's Lace, for example, can be beautiful. Emotional weeds, too—for example, false impressions of ourself—can have a contributory impact on our life if they serve to some extent as positive compost fuel, that is, if the suffering caused by the weeds helps us define how we want to treat others in contrast to how we were regarded and treated as children. This can contribute to wonderful growth and a beautiful blossoming of our persons. However, emotional weeds usually—and unconsciously so—can choke out our experience of the good within us.

Notes

All of us will at some time or another experience the weeds as both positive compost fuel and as unconscious intruders. It happens in different order for different people, and whether positive compost fuel or unconscious blockers, they alternate constantly throughout life. However, the challenge and the opportunity for every person is to learn how to use the weeds for fuel *and* how to manage them when they crop up and block the flow of the person's natural and good self.

Because of the individual garden that every person is, we've each had emotional weeds within us for a long time. They were planted within us early in life, are deeply rooted, and at some point, will be persistent in cropping up. Getting ever more limber in our awareness of these deeply planted weeds is how we pull them each and every time.

We have no idea how many weeds—moments of false beliefs about ourself, the world, and life—were planted in us. So, our commitment to self must be to use our awareness to keep catching and pulling these weeds whenever they crop up. These baffling, unsettling, demoralizing, even terrifying weeds are indeed persistent in their cropping up, but they are *not* part of the actual soil or fabric of who we are.

> *These baffling, unsettling, demoralizing,*
> *even terrifying weeds are persistent in their cropping up,*
> *but they are <u>not</u> part of the actual soil or fabric of who we are.*

<u>Example</u>. *During a summertime ten years ago, you ate some cherries, swallowed one with the pit still inside, and the pit lodged in your stomach. After these ten years, it caused a stomach bleed and then discharged itself. That cherry pit had lived in you for ten years.*

Did you ever become the cherry pit? No, you didn't. Was that cherry pit stored in you for a long time and, when it was coming out, cause some difficulty? Yes, that's true. The cherry pit was not consciously impacting you for a long time, but then it did start to cause physical distress. You will have to deal with the impact of the cherry pit that lived in you for so long, but this intruding substance never became you.

This is also true of the baffling, difficult, childhood messages we received about ourself, about the world, about life—emotional weeds that were planted in us.

Notes

We have been told by well-intentioned writers, speakers, and teachers that if we do this or that, if we take this approach or that approach, we will be able to find a weed-free peace in our lives. While the intentions voiced in this regard are sincere and caring, it's unfair to give anyone the impression that the unpacking of childhood bafflement—which, for a child, is trauma—is not a lifelong process.

It's unfair to give anyone the impression that the right mindset or technique can act like emotional weed killer or to suggest that, with the right frame of mind, we have the power to keep these weeds from cropping up, or that we can immediately stop whatever pain has cropped up like a weed in our emotional garden, cropped up through no fault or doing of our own.

Just as emotional heat and warmth today can defrost anything in our childhood freezer, heat and warmth—seemingly out of nowhere—can also cause the weeds planted in us early in life to crop up today, something that will happen now and again throughout our life.

Just as it is our personal responsibility and daily promise to ourself to stay fed and hydrated, it's our personal responsibility to:

- recognize the weeds that crop up in our emotional gardens,
- use our awareness as the garden tool for digging around and then pulling these weeds by the root,
- identity where they come from, and
- remember that they're not an inherent part of the garden of who we each are and that they will return to varying degrees throughout our lifetime.

Our minds do indeed have the power to develop limber emotional reflexes which can catch when these weeds intrude into our life. And our minds have the power to develop the emotional muscle to then pull, hold, listen to, and understand these pieces of our early life experience. There will forever be additional installments from the subconscious parts of our autobiography.

However, the cropping up of these weeds cannot be stopped. It's unfair to suggest to someone that these weeds should be stopped and that there's a skill we can learn which will do so.

Notes

We will remain much fairer to, respectful of, and humane with ourself if through our brave awareness:

- We keep our emotional reflexes limber to catch the weeds from our childhood each time they crop up.
- We keep our emotional muscles strong to pull, hold, recognize, and sort through these weeds for what they are.

As they continue to crop up throughout life, we can indeed stay on top of the weeds—as annoying as it may be to do so—if we are willing to do so each time. The more limber we get at recognizing these weeds for what they are and where they come from, the more quickly we will diffuse them, the more skilled we'll be at keeping our garden weeded, and the more fully we will own our life story.

Notes

6. Navigation/Survival Strategies

Children have an unbelievable, unconscious, instinctive, and natural ability to craft navigation/survival strategies for what troubles, unsettles, confuses, and even scares them about a parent, the household into which they are born, and the nuclear and wider family of which they find themself a member. There are many such strategies for navigating and surviving the at-home trauma that a child experiences—whether consciously or not. However, they all fall under one umbrella strategy for survival that has many variations: *ceasing to exist*.

Two clear examples of *ceasing to exist* include:

- when a person takes their life through suicide or by unconsciously losing themself in some other way, and

- when an individual feels like they don't exist and then—consciously or not—takes another person's life through murder or some form of destroying a person's spirit, an unconscious way of asking someone to share their feeling of not existing, of asking someone to keep them company by ceasing to exist.

There is an endless array of things people do in their lives that can serve the purpose of ceasing to exist. Childhood versions of not existing include:

1. hiding;

2. running away from home;

3. shyness and super-shyness;

4. using defiance as an act of protection for oneself (so the real self doesn't have to exist / be present and can stay protected within);

5. getting lost in academics, sports, gaming of one kind or another, reading books or magazines, using social media;

6. not doing homework; and

7. excessive sleeping.

Notes

And there are more. By not existing either literally or metaphorically, a child can feel invisible or detached and, as a result, feel safer in life.

In adult life, the strategy of the child someone once was—the strategy of not existing in order to be safe—continues unconsciously so, but with a variety of costumes. This partial list of examples calls for a slow reading of them:

1-7. any of the childhood versions noted on the previous page;

8. having no opinion;

9. lacking self-esteem;

10. never speaking up;

11. never enjoying a peaceful self (because experiencing a peaceful self had to be put on hold due to having to navigate devaluing regard and treatment by a parent, sibling, or someone else);

12. living on guard (living on yellow, orange, or red alert);

13. using bravado as a way to fake some power and keep our real self safe within;

14. disappearing into others, their opinions, their wants;

15. erasing ourself by always apologizing;

16. violence against self;

17. violence against others (physical, sexual, emotional) so they, too, would cease to exist or at least exist in a lessened way;

18. wishing that another individual or even whole groups of people (based on race, ethnicity, religion, sexual self-identity) did not exist, again asking someone or many others to keep oneself company by not existing;

19. substance abuse and disappearing into an addiction;

Notes

20. holding our breath to one degree or another at almost all times without consciously knowing it (because we never knew what was going to happen next at home);

21. keeping excessive work hours;

22. doing all the work in whatever situation or relationship;

23. doing the bare minimum (for example, having a job but then when at home doing nothing but sit on the couch);

24. not keeping a job;

25. being driven by image, status, or title;

26. not maintaining a home free of dirt and/or clutter, maybe even hoarding, that is, not existing by getting lost in the mess;

27. not maintaining bodily or dental hygiene;

28. carrying excessive weight;

29. being a lazy thinker (not thinking things through, letting someone else's mind think instead of our own—be this a family member or, in some cases, via a set of religious or social beliefs);

30. hiding our true self by demonstrating/wearing the behaviors of someone else (usually "wearing" the behavior of a parent to feel connected to them—even if it's logically counterproductive to ourself to do so);

31. sexual dysfunction;

32. dating or returning to date someone who devalues (abuses) us physically, sexually, mentally, or emotionally;

33. staying up late because it's the first time each day we might feel free to exist;

34. waiting for each event, including each day, to end;

35. having an affinity with death (for example, finding great peace in death, maybe enjoying funerals, perhaps engaging in death-defying activities);

Notes

36. professionally living a life of service in which one gets *buried*; and

37. living as if the truth didn't exist, as if the truth wasn't the truth (for example, making reputable sources into liars, or saying that how a group of people is treated over time doesn't become woven into the fabric of how a society continues to regard and treat such a group).

These last examples of individuals wanting the truth to not exist are rooted in a pervasive fear about the truth of their parent's negative impact on them during childhood because, once someone genuinely commits to the truth, that commitment will begin to impact all dimensions of their life.

It will include individuals finally having to own the truth about the less-than-positive impacts of their parents and family members on them. "Honor Your Father and Mother" once again is at the core of someone's fear about the truth. Justice for others is a threat if justice for yourself through truth is too terrifying.

> *Justice for others is a threat*
> *if justice for yourself through truth is too terrifying.*

Each of the examples of not existing listed above is a stance toward life that we'd enthusiastically support anyone shifting away from in order to adjust their life for the better. However, these *ceasing to exist* strategies started with good reason, for example:

- never speaking up in order to not incur the humiliation of someone belittling what we said, the humiliation of someone belittling us;

- believing that ceasing to exist in some way would correct our "mistake" of being an intrusion, a burden, or an "oops" to our parents, that is, make us a good person rather than the bad person we feel like we are; and

- making ourself the person who was doing something wrong (meanness, lack of personal responsibility including self-care, substance use, and more) in lieu of conscious awareness of—raw knowing about—how wrong a parent might have been in some ways, especially regarding the things we needed them to do for us that would not have cost them a penny.

Notes

Yes, each variation of the strategy of ceasing to exist started with good reason: survival. It's just that a navigation/survival lifeboat sized for a child will either sink each time an adult steps into it, or it will capsize, flip up, and land on the person's head.

Ceasing to exist can be used beneficially at times.

Example. You have a manager who is the only one allowed to exist at work, the one who claims all the spotlight, all the credit. In this case, "not existing" could be a smart stance to take if you were going to stay at this job.

But ceasing to exist is not what anyone wants threaded through their life 24/7.

Because the *ceasing to exist* navigation/survival strategies started with good reason—to protect the child someone once was, ourself included—it's important to retire these strategies by honoring the service they once provided. We may be annoyed with and weary of them to whatever degree they are still active, but they started in one form or another with the positive intention to carry us through childhood. And they did just that. Awareness of this will give the various ways we might not exist honorable retirements day by day, a little bit more each day.

As we give honor to the unconscious creativity that was ours—which is *not* in any way giving honor to how we were hurt, how we may have hurt ourself, how we may have hurt someone else by any acting out—it won't be arduous work to determine, commission, and engage in one or several new life navigation strategies. They will surface on their own from the innate creativity in each of us to manage life effectively—and they will serve us naturally and well.

> *New life navigation strategies will surface on their own from the innate creativity in each of us to manage life effectively —and they will serve us naturally and well.*

As life progresses, if we unconsciously remain in the lifeboat that served us so well as a child, we will be adrift with behaviors and emotions active today but dictated by the childhood sea through which we once had to navigate.

Notes

However, by using our awareness, we can shift from being someone adrift in an old and small lifeboat, someone buffeted each day by the old childhood sea. We can instead be on a train steaming forward and powered by a fuel that we'll forever have at our disposal: the fuel of being aware.

Over time, this will let us stay out of the lifeboat that once saved us and instead find ourself on a train that will take us into new physical, sexual, intellectual, and emotional places in our life.

"Out of the lifeboat and onto the train." And we'll enjoy the journey.

Notes

7. Literal Language Telling the Truth

The language we use day-to-day is amazingly helpful both in understanding what's going on inside of us and in understanding why working through things in life can be so difficult. Collectively, we have unconsciously used many phrases which say so much, but we've unconsciously hidden behind them rather than truly identify the truth they hold for us. Here are two examples.

Beside Myself

Although this concept was already addressed in the essay "Struggle versus Challenge," it's important enough to include it again and recap it here. Feeling *beside myself* is often described as experiencing great confusion, swirling with helplessness, frantic, not knowing what to do, and struggling—to name a few examples. However, we are really being quite precise.

Struggling is when something happening today has defrosted something from our childhood emotional freezer or caused a weed planted in childhood by a parent or family member to crop up again. The meeting of the two emotional fronts of today and early life becomes a violent swirling within us—or between us and someone else—just as when there is a meteorological tornado within which people, buildings, vehicles, nature itself, literally everything gets caught up in the swirl of the wind and is violently impacted.

Feeling beside myself is an indicator of just such a struggle, indicator of an emotional tornado. What we are feeling in one of these experiences are the exact feelings that were ours in childhood. As these defrosted feelings and early life weeds arrive today in the form of struggle, we are in those very moments, literally beside the childhood self we once were. We are feeling LTCIOW: like the child I once was. We feel beside ourself, and metaphorically, we're right.

> *We are feeling LTCIOW.*
> *We feel beside ourself, and metaphorically, we're right.*

Notes

As our personal awareness catches this dynamic, the tornado—the frozen feelings and cropped-up weeds from our childhood triggered loose by some type of emotional heat or warmth today—will quiet down. Feeling beside myself will subside, and we'll return to experiencing our true and natural self of today.

Beside myself is truer than most of us ever realized, and what a helpful and important realization to have.

Acting Out

Quite often when we are affronted or taken aback by our own or someone else's behaviors, attitudes, or words, most of us have said something like:

- "What was that all about?"

- "Where did that come from?"

- "That makes no sense."

We may follow these questions and comments with a statement such as "Well, they're certainly acting out today," or with the question "What was I just acting out?" Our verbiage is uncanny in its accuracy. We may think the issue is the inappropriate behavior of today, but this behavior is the costume for an old childhood story.

There are three ways we get the stories of childhood confusion, pain, and hurt out of us. The first two are conscious choices.

We may intentionally write out the story by putting pen to paper whether in personal notes for ourself (referred to earlier in "As Basic as One, Two, Three"), or by intentionally writing a letter or using online messaging to connect with someone. We may talk it out with a family member, friend, colleague, helping professional, or some other confidant. Regarding others, we will often encourage someone who seems troubled to do one or both of these: to write it out and/or talk it out.

The third way we get frozen childhood pain out of us is an unconscious one. We may act it out. *Out* is the key word here. Whether consciously or not, we want to get our childhood pain *out* from within ourself.

Notes

When we don't have conscious words for what our system wants to get out from our childhood emotional freezer, when the pain is too great for words, when perhaps we're too afraid to face whatever is churning within us, when too much unconscious energy is being used to either carry the frozen pain within, stomp out the weeds, or divert us from either, our whole system takes over and gets it out by unconsciously acting it out.

> *When the pain is too great for words, our whole system takes over and gets it out by unconsciously acting it out.*

Much of what gets acted out is from when we were pre-verbal and didn't have the ability to use words to get things out. It's also from those times when we did have access to words, but we'd be punished for expressing our thoughts and feelings. In either case, we flash froze those moments, feelings, and words.

When we talk something out, our main goal is to get someone to understand what we're experiencing. We'll have a conversation if we want someone to intellectually get what we're sharing. However, when we unconsciously want someone to *feel* what we're describing, we add some drama to our words—also unconsciously. That's when our communication becomes *acting out* communication.

The first communication from most of us was acted out. Very often when a baby is born in a hospital, the very first thing the baby does upon leaving their parent's womb is to cry—even scream. The baby is acting out in distress because they viscerally know these things: "I'm no longer in the safe darkness of my parent's womb. Instead, I'm in a cold room with bright lights with strangers holding me." Why wouldn't someone express their distress at such a contrast of experiences? And by way of their distressed shout-outs, the baby gets us to feel their distress to some degree, too.

At birth, a baby has no inhibitions about expressing their distress, and at times during their life as a baby, they will continue to do so. However, the baby soon learns to be cautious about being expressive. More and more of what baffles and pains a baby—perhaps confusion, hurt, fear—starts to be flash frozen and stored within because with increasing frequency the baby is discouraged from being expressive with either words or emotions.

Notes

As life proceeds, "stuff" that's been stored by the baby and then by the child we were wants to come out. Because it's so often frowned upon when a child does let something out, starting early in life and continuing into adulthood, most of us revert—unconsciously so and in varying degrees—to the form of communication to which we first had access at birth and by which our words won't get dismissed, devalued, or punished. We unconsciously begin to communicate through acting out.

Again, the unconscious purpose of acting out something is to get someone to not just intellectually understand what we want to communicate but also to get them to feel it, specifically to feel the story of what we had lived through as a child. By doing so, we unconsciously get someone to keep us company, to give us the unconscious comfort that we're not alone in these feelings, and to provide the comfort that someone now really knows something we've been feeling—consciously or not—forever. We finally get some type of response to our conscious or unconscious and forever longing to be seen, known, and understood.

Isn't that always the purpose of effective acting whether it's on the stage, in a movie, or on television? Good acting gets us to not only know a story, but it also gets us to feel it. That's why when we leave a good and well-acted stage or screen performance, we first talk about how it made us feel—happy, scared, creeped out, disgusted, sad, peaceful, inspired, aware—and then we discuss the storyline itself.

This is also why music has such an impact on us. It's a type of acting, a performance. Whether it's the blasting of cannons within the "1812 Overture" (Tchaikovsky), the match-up of words and music in a national anthem, songs such as "Climb Every Mountain" (Rogers and Hammerstein) or "What a Wonderful World" (Louis Armstrong), music adds an experience of feeling the story being told. When something is acted out, the full force of the message is not only heard, it's felt, it's experienced.

However, when someone is acting out, it's very hard for the receiver of the story to immediately engage with it and receive it with some level of objectivity. The person acting out unconsciously wants someone to know and feel what they've been struggling with, and so they are making the receiver of their story struggle, too. If the story's receiver is being caught up into the drama of the story-teller's struggle—buffeted by the content and emotions of the story—how difficult it truly is to find one's footing and collect clues, decode, interpret, and translate the message of the story being acted out.

Notes

So, how can we anchor ourselves and figure out the story being communicated? Over time we can develop the skill to do our decoding work in real-time while a story is being acted out. However, as we begin using this skill, we'll be practicing it after-the-fact for quite a while, and debriefing it, when we can step back out of the drama.

Here's how we can do the debrief:

1. We first listen to the words we are using to describe how the person was acting, for example: controlling, calling the shots, beside themself, out of control, impressed with themself, unsure, hard on themself, inappropriate, and many others. It will help to write these down so that we can see the words and use them as puzzle pieces to be fit together.

2. We then gather additional puzzle pieces: We identify how the storyteller is making *us* feel. Perhaps this is scared, sad, helpless, hopeless, lost, confused, worthless, and more. It helps to write these down as well.

With the descriptions of the storyteller's behavior/acting + the feelings we are unconsciously being asked to feel, we will be able to fit a few puzzle pieces together and arrive at some degree of understanding about what this person is communicating.

> *So, how do we figure out the story being communicated?*
> *We describe how the storyteller is acting.*
> *We then identify how the storyteller is making us feel.*

Here are several examples:

Example 1. A child is making a parent feel terribly disrespected by seeming to care nothing about the impact of their disrespectful actions on their parent. Perhaps the parent will realize that they themself did something—unaware of it as they were at the time—that made their child feel disrespected. It could have been a flippant comment. It could have been how embarrassed the parent made the child feel in front of friends because the parent was being inappropriate in some way due to anger or alcohol.

Even if something happened only once, it had a searing impact of disrespect on the child and is being acted out now. The child is unconsciously asking their parent to struggle with what it feels like to be disrespected by someone close to them.

Notes

Example 2. *A person is acting as if they are worth nothing by not keeping their apartment clean or by misusing substances. Or they may be treating other people as if they are worth nothing.*

Perhaps this person viscerally—not intellectually—felt like they were worth nothing at birth because the person who had carried them in their womb for so many months put them up for adoption, that is, gave them away. Every child knows that things that are worth nothing are given away or thrown out. This is another example of something that happened to the child only once but had a baffling, beyond words impact, and is now being acted out. This person is telling the story of what it's like to struggle with feeling like you're worth nothing.

Example 3. *A parent, sibling, or other family member is in an altered state one day and randomly begins shooting a gun in the backyard. Although the person was out of control and had no responsible awareness of what they were doing, you would never forget an experience like this. You would forever be afraid of this person to some degree and live on yellow, orange, or even red alert with them. Things would never be quite the same for you.*

The person shooting the gun is communicating a story about having once been made so afraid during childhood by someone out of control and who had no awareness of what they were doing physically, sexually, or emotionally, that things were never quite the same for them. You now have some understanding that the gun-shooting family member has forever lived on yellow, orange, or even red alert because you are also now struggling with feeling afraid and with having no control—like the person shooting the gun once had to feel.

Example 4. *A person may routinely "call all the shots," use abusive language, use substances counterproductively, drive recklessly, or be defiant with their life partner, with siblings, even with law enforcement. Whether consciously remembered or not, perhaps this person was once helpless to call the shots when being sexually abused during childhood by a parent, sibling, or someone else, whether once or often.*

The message they are shouting—acting out—in any number of ways today is, "No one is ever again going to make me do anything I don't want to do. I'm going to call the shots in my life." In calling all the shots, this person is asking others to struggle with feeling totally helpless—like the person once so tragically had to feel when being sexually abused.

It is tiring indeed whenever someone continues to act out, when we have to keep decoding this type of communication. However, when we invest time in decoding,

---

Notes

interpreting, deciphering, determining what someone is trying to communicate by what they act out, several things may happen.

First, the decoding benefits the one doing the decoding. You identify the clues of the story—that is, how the person was acting and how you were made to feel by the acting out. Even though you may or may not know the precise details of the story:

- You'll have some level of understanding of what had happened to the person.

- You'll know some of the old emotions stored in that person's childhood emotional freezer or some of the weeds of false belief once planted in them.

Now that you know to some degree the awful feelings that this person had to experience at one or more points in their early life—without you doing anything conscious or specific—it will change how you feel inside, soften the look on your face, adjust the tone in your voice so it's gentle or firm in just the right way, in short, give you better footing and voice for what you are navigating. The person acting out won't be aware of this consciously, but their radar will pick up on it.

Second, it benefits the one acting out. Having their acting out decoded will help the one acting out to *unconsciously* feel *listened to* by someone. They'll be the recipient of a new form of the concept of active listening. This new active listening is not limited to written words nor words verbalized within a conversation. It's listening that could be described as a *private understanding* of what someone is acting out.

It may not happen immediately that the one acting out will unconsciously feel listened to, but it's indeed likely that the person or group acting out—at some point and to some degree—will have unconsciously felt heard. Although not conscious, the "game" being played through acting out is, "I won't listen to you unless I sense that you have listened to me."

> *Although not conscious,*
> *the "game" being played through acting out is,*
> *"I won't listen to you*
> *unless I sense that you have listened to me."*

Notes

People act out all the time. In the workplace, a response by a manager to someone's acting out has to be based on specific feedback, feedback focused on the employee's compliance or non-compliance with the performance standards laid out for the person's work or for their membership on their work team.

Private understanding—that something not work-related is impacting the employee's performance, as general and non-specific as it might be—can't be directly addressed by the manager. It's not appropriate to do so in the workplace. However, it can help the manager be better grounded in their interactions with the employee because a broader perspective becomes part of the manager's awareness.

Private understanding of what someone is acting out can be used with an aggravating neighbor or co-worker, even with some members of one's extended family. However, the extra energy it takes to do private understanding, this decoding and interpreting, is best invested for those in our innermost circle, most especially for a life partner, or when a parent is trying to understand and provide direction for their child, or when the relationship is an important friendship.

It would be impossible to engage the skills of private understanding with everyone we encounter who is acting out. However, understanding the concept will alert us to what we're up against in certain situations, and it will make us aware that something beyond logic is at play.

Private understanding of any acting out by our life partner, child, or good friend is not only worth doing, it's a requirement because of the importance of such a relationship. It will always benefit both us and them if we engage private understanding skills with those whom we value the most in our life.

It will also benefit us all if, in general, we use the word *communicating* rather than always using the words *talking* or *telling*. Talking/telling imposes a limit on the form of communication to talking it out. Communication in general is intended to get it out. We will become more skilled at communicating in direct proportion to how we improve our understanding that there are three forms of communication:

Writing It Out
Self-processing: Someone intentionally expressing to themself or to someone else via the written word

---

Notes

Talking It Out
Interactive processing: One person consciously expressing things in words and another person listening and possibly responding

Acting It Out
Outsourcing the processing: Someone unconsciously asks another person to decode, interpret, translate, and understand their acting out. Optimally, if it can all be discussed at some point, the person acting out can then self-responsibly reflect on what they've acted out, come to understand it, and manage it themself going forward rather than distressing and burdening the receiver with figuring out the story.

Deciphering someone's *Acting It Out* communication is indeed draining work, even annoying work. Why should any of us have to work that hard to understand someone? Why can't they simply explain their thoughts and feelings to us in words, in a conversation?

It's so important to remember that whatever is being acted out is being communicated unconsciously, without conscious strategy or planning. It's something the communicator doesn't even know they're doing. It's something from the person's childhood freezer—or a weed planted during childhood—that's too painful to consciously realize, let alone verbalize. But it's something the person's system wants to get out from where it's been stored for such a very long time.

There are two reasons why acting out may continue repeatedly:

First, it may be because the story being acted out happened many times, even countless times in the life of the storyteller. It may seem like the same thing being acted out over and over, but because the storyteller had to endure and store the experience many times, it's a new installment of the story coming out each time.

Second, the repetition of the acting out may be a variation on a theme of an old cell phone commercial. Trying to test the connection power of the cell service, someone was pictured making a call from the jungle and asking, "Can you hear me now?" Or from a tunnel, "Can you hear me now?" Or in a blinding and howling storm and yelling, "CAN YOU HEAR ME NOW?!?"

In addition to individuals unconsciously acting out their stored childhood pain, childhood stories are also acted out collectively by groups of people. It's always more difficult

---

Notes

to apply private understanding when it's a group doing the acting out. However, such private understanding will still facilitate our having greater perspective and better footing for what we are navigating regarding that group or situation.

Example. A group of people has found connection and energy with each other as they campaign for a cause. If their commitment to the cause seems energized to a frightening degree, the over-animation is the costume for an unconsciously strong desire to obtain something very important to them—perhaps feeling connected, having value, knowing personal dignity. As a united front, they believe that they finally have the chance to achieve one or all of these purposes, and they want the energy of feeling powerful as they work toward their goal.

On the road to getting what they want, they may intimidate others by stoking fear or hate. Logical explanation of any facts contrary to their cause doesn't have a snowball's chance of surviving their heated drives. The truth doesn't matter to them. No one is going to take away the access to victory which they feel is close at hand. In fact, the cause against which they fight with such intimidating tactics is almost always a cause similar to their own: what another group of people is doing to find their own sense of connection, value, and dignity.

The unconscious solidarity that the group of warriors has found with each other is likely this: as children they had no power over anything and could exert no influence over the situation in which they each found themselves—environments in which they were denied connection, value, and dignity—and they each hated it. They routinely felt frustrated, helpless, even hopeless. They were intimidated and terrified by the oppressive childhood reality that was theirs.

So, other groups fighting for relief from their own particular oppression from childhood or otherwise—a child's feeling less than, powerless, unsure regarding their sexual orientation or gender identity, someone oppressed by income inequality, race, or gender—are reminding the united warriors of their own unconscious pain when growing up. The warriors are therefore shouting to any others fighting for relief from oppression, "Stop reminding us of our own lifelong pain and oppression! Stop diverting us from what we want to finally get for ourselves!"

The united warriors therefore collectively resent and even hate anyone fighting for relief from whatever form of oppression. Other groups fighting for relief from oppression become a danger to the warriors, a threat to stirring up an awareness of the warriors' own early life pain. The united warriors perceive such personal awareness—not as something that can help them to finally be honest with themselves about the emotionally difficult lives, the

---

Notes

truly difficult lives, they had to navigate as children—but as an obstacle to their gaining access to the connection, value, and dignity they are so close to finally winning.

The group of warriors has aligned around their unconscious childhood stories, not really the cause they're fighting for, and they are acting out the awful pain they had to endure as children. They are unconsciously—but actively—making others know and feel the earliest experience of life that was theirs: frustrated, helpless, and hopeless regarding their access to connection, value, and dignity.

Observers of the group of warriors can struggle with how to respond, feeling "beside themselves" in the situation. This indicates that the observers' own childhood stories left them feeling frustrated, helpless, hopeless, and even terrified to whatever degree. It's only with full awareness of these swirling dynamics that the intimidated, terrified party can find their creative voice and footing to interact with those so driven to be at war and win.

Whether an individual person or a group, those who act out are unconsciously waiting for someone to listen, hear, and privately understand their innermost pain from childhood. There's a good possibility that when the person or group acting out feels heard—even though it's an unconscious awareness of being heard—they will dial down the acting out and even dial up their willingness to hear whatever the receiver of their communication has to say to them.

> *There's a good possibility that when the person or group acting out feels heard, they will dial down the acting out and even dial up their willingness to hear whatever the receiver of their communication has to say to them.*

Beside myself. Acting out. Words worth understanding literally.

Notes

8. "Bad" Words

Usually when we talk about "bad" words we are talking about four-letter words: hell, s***, f***, and more. However, some of the most dangerous four-letter words are ones that we use often. They are words which do us harm, words by which we do injustice to ourself more than we might realize, words which take us away from the truth and leave us pretending. And the promise we each want to make to ourself is *telling the truth, and no more pretending.*

The observations you are about to read are about some common—yet counterproductive—uses of language, observations which may surprise you, given the prominence of certain words and their use. Here are some examples of "bad" words.

Need

The word *need* may be the most dangerous word in anyone's vocabulary. It has a recurring place in our thinking and speaking, in our personal life, and in our professional life, too. The famous phrase *hierarchy of needs* and the word *need* itself have become pervasive in ordinary understanding and in everyday communication.

The word *need* is present in individual counseling as professionals help their clients determine values, set goals, and identify their needs. It is present in marriage counseling when life partners are asked to identify what they need from each other, when they are encouraged to be as responsive as possible to a partner's needs. Work supervisors say things to their direct reports like, "I need to have such and such by this afternoon." Television characters tell one another what they need from each other. Those in positions of political leadership talk about "what we all need to do."

It's quite stunning to notice how often we hear people use the word *need* and how often we use the word in our self-talk about whatever there is to do or feel, for example:

- "I need to get this done today."
- "I need to feel appreciated."
- "I need to talk to them."
- "I need them to understand me."

Notes

Need by definition means...

- I can't do it without...
- I can't live without...

...two phrases that are quite desperate and which imply a life-and-death dependence on someone or something even if the situation isn't one of life or death.

It's true that *children* are in such a dependent place of need as their life begins, because it's life-and-death for a child to have:

- physical safety through proper nutrition, a secure place to live, and non-violent discipline;

- intellectual safety through appropriate education, learning, and understanding;

- sexual safety from body-related impropriety and devaluing of any kind and to whatever degree; and

- emotional safety such that a child feels nourished to be and treasured as the individual they are.

If these early life needs are not being met by a parent, a dependent place for a child becomes a desperate place for them, and it often continues as a desperate life for them as an adult.

Every person is also in such a dependent place of need during a serious medical situation and at the conclusion of their life because these are life-and-death situations. Everyone is in a place of need when their physical well-being and safety are threatened due to lack of food and water, and because of exposure to danger and violence. We might say that "we need to do our taxes," but even in this case it only feels like life-and-death if not doing them could land us in prison.

Because a child can't do so many things without a parent—can't live without a parent, or because someone may be unable to care for themselves as they are navigating a health crisis, or because well-being and safety are threatened by some type of violence or danger—these are all needs because they are life-and-death situations.

Notes

Needs are life-and-death situations.

Children uniquely have physical and emotional needs, especially the need for emotional safety: the safety of feeling good about themself, feeling nourished and treasured as the individual they are. All needs as life progresses from there are based on physical requirements to sustain life and be safe. We can live without a specific set of emotions or feelings. We can live without sexual experiences. Hermits have survived in their seclusion throughout the history of the world. However, we can't live without food, water, and physical safety.

When we use the word *need*, we immediately put ourselves into *a dependent place*, perhaps even into *a desperate state of mind and heart*. When we experience ourself thinking the word *need*, it feels heavy with dependence, desperation, or both. When we're dependent, we lack confidence and can't find our footing. When we're desperate, we're so afraid and frantic—whether consciously or not—that we're temporarily unable to find perspective or connection with anything or anyone, not even with ourself.

The *hierarchy of needs* has been helpful to identify what's important in our lives. However, except for the physical needs of food, water, medical care, and feeling safe while walking down the street or flying in an airplane—physical survival requirements— adults don't have needs.

*Except for the physical needs of food, water, medical care,
and feeling safe—physical survival requirements—
adults don't have needs.*

With the exception of the examples just noted, there is nothing that an adult can't do without or can't live without. There are many things that someone might like to have in their life, find important for their life, might even find critical for their life, but none other than food, water, and physical safety are needs. Someone might even have a lack of interpersonal emotional connection in life; but even when this is missing, there is much emotion that can be found through music, in nature, and via additional sources.

Notes

However, CHILDREN DO HAVE NEEDS. They have physical, intellectual, sexual safety, and emotional needs because they can't *do it without* or *live without* unless these needs are filled first by a parent. Other people—siblings or adults—may fill in some of the gaps, but the gaps left by a parent not filling their child's needs has a lifelong and recurring impact.

When someone talks about what they need from another person (intimate partner, child, friend, neighbor, co-worker, manager), they often feel like they are going in circles because the request being made is most likely not a physical survival requirement. It can feel like a no-win situation. Conversations about what one needs may deliver a short-term solution, but there will be no shelf-life for it.

If a parent who is charged with fulfilling the needs of a child missed their chance, it's like a hole is left in that person for life. It will sting with pain now and again forever. It will never go away. The hole won't be Grand Canyon-sized, but it will always be there, flaring up off and on. This is the impact left by a need not met in childhood by a parent. It's another way to describe a pain we had to flash freeze during childhood to survive it, freezing it so we could proceed with our day, with our life, or to describe a weed planted early in our life by a parent or family member.

It's each person's responsibility across life to stay limber enough to catch when one of the holes of their unmet childhood needs is enflamed. Once identified, it must be processed for what it is—the residual sting of an unmet childhood need—rather than getting quickly trapped in the narrow and false presumption that the pain is about what we have routinely thought of as a need today.

The word *need* works against us in several ways:

- When we tell ourselves that "we need to do something," we often won't do it. We unconsciously make the *something* to be done too big. We make it daunting—unconsciously make it life-and-death—and end up paralyzing ourself.

- When we tell ourself that "we need something" from someone else, we have unconsciously made what we'd like to experience from them so big that nothing someone might do in response will feel like enough to us.

- When we tell someone else what "we need from them," our request may be *unconsciously* received as a life-and-death request. Unconsciously, the other

---

Notes

82

person feels, "This is too big," or "This is impossible." So, they unconsciously back off from trying to be responsive. Or the request is unconsciously received as something only a parent could have provided. This isn't too big for someone other than a parent to deliver on. It's impossible to deliver on for the person being asked.

Examples of language that keep us from getting caught up in a sense of life-and-death include:

- "This is something I *want*."

- "This is *important* to me."

- "It *means a lot* to me."

- "This is *critical* for me."

The right language can free someone of whom we're making a request to have some agency of response.

> *Language can keep us from getting caught up in a sense of life-and-death. And it frees someone of whom we're making a request to have some agency of response.*

Other than what's life-and-death physically, intellectually, regarding sexual safety, and emotionally in a child's life...

Other than the life-and-death situation that's potentially the end of life...

Other than each person's medical and physical safety throughout life...

...we don't have needs.

Need can be an energizing word when it comes to responding appropriately and with urgency to the very real dependencies of a child or of someone in medical distress. It can be an energizing word if we find ourself in a burning building, for example, "I need to get out of here," or "I need to get them out of here."

Notes

However, the word *need* is usually a paralyzing word. It's quite often unfair to ourself to use it, and it's unfair for us to use the word with anyone to whom we are looking for support and care in life. Being especially aware of this word and using it only where appropriate will let each of us feel more peaceful. It will let each of us and others exercise our agency more effectively and naturally.

Heal

A great disservice has been done by helping professionals who use the word *heal* regarding our painful emotions. The word comes from a physical health model where things can and do heal (even though some sort of scar or impact may remain). Using the word *heal* regarding our emotional self is as inappropriate as has been the concept of medications carried over to an excessive degree from the medical world into the world of emotions and psychology.

The painful bafflements from our childhood emotional history are addressed bit by bit over time as they defrost, as we unpack them, as we pull the weeds from childhood that have a lifetime warranty and will forever crop up. When we use the words *heal* or *healed* when it comes to emotions, we become non-productively harsh with ourself. We feel like we're failing or not doing something right when more of our old, frozen emotions thaw out and surface for unpacking, when those weeds planted early in life return. We can unfairly be asking ourselves, "What am I not doing right? What am I doing wrong that I have not yet healed?"

Through our awareness, it is indeed possible for us to:

- navigate the emotions from our childhood emotional freezer when they defrost, and
- pull the weeds planted during childhood when they crop up today.

Our commitment to doing this will bring about more and more *healing*, but healing when it comes to emotions is an *ongoing process*, not an end. It will continue a bit more all along the way—forever.

There is no way to ever say that my emotional freezer is now emptied and that its contents will no longer bother me. There's no patented emotional weed killer to ensure that the emotional weeds planted in childhood won't crop up. Leaks from our childhood

Notes

emotional freezer and weeds cropping up again from childhood do not mean we're not doing something right about how we're handling our emotions.

As was addressed in the essay "The Baffling Pain of Childhood," if during just one day in childhood, across our sixteen waking hours, we flash froze ten nanoseconds of baffling, scary, or hurtful moments that we didn't know what to do with—or moments when we were consciously or unconsciously aware of weeds being planted in us—in just one year of childhood we could have stored 3,650 such moments within us. After ten years, we could have an estimated 36,000+ such moments in storage. And this number is most likely on the low end.

These moments went in one at a time, and they will come out, thaw, defrost, crop up one by one across a lifetime, and there is no magic way to empty our childhood emotional freezer or blast away the weeds planted during childhood. There is no emotional surgery or vacuum that can warp-speed dealing with any of this.

Each stored moment holds within it an impact on us of how we experienced life as a child. So, our emotional system is, in truth. being truly kind to us by spreading out in installments its presenting of our autobiography, the experiences and feelings that have been stored within our emotional freezer or that crop up like weeds. The process of sorting through all this is called healing. Its promise is ever more healing, never "healed."

> *Each stored moment holds within it an impact on us*
> *of how we experienced life as a child.*
> *The process of sorting through all this is called healing.*
> *Its promise is ever more healing, never "healed."*

For one, there's too much volume-wise for anyone to bear in any single release of information and the accompanying emotions. For another, the pain that is there was stored for a reason: it was hurtful, it was heavy, and it was scary. Moments were experienced and frozen—or planted—one at a time, and they'll defrost or crop up one at a time, too, a mirror of each time something was frozen or planted.

Anything we feel that doesn't make sense is coming from somewhere, and that somewhere is either our childhood emotional freezer or from among the weeds planted by a

Notes

parent or family members. Managing our old, frozen, childhood emotions when they thaw out and navigating the weeds from childhood that crop up are both possible. Being healed of them completely—or free of them forever—is not.

Managing our old, frozen, childhood emotions when they thaw out and navigating the weeds from childhood that crop up are both possible. Being healed of them completely—or free of them forever—is not.

Bit by bit, we proceed through life coming to know with ever greater consciousness—as much as possible—what happened to us, what we lived through, what we had to navigate as children. This is how we own our life story and live as people of integrity, live as people owning our own individual truth. It's also what gives us the context for where "stuff is coming from" in our life today. More truth-owning means more healing.

Hope

Another word that can often be a "bad" word is the word *hope*. Hope doesn't produce magic. It can't make things come about that simply can't happen. If you ordered something online but it's out of stock, hope can't produce the product for you by the next day even if you paid for overnight delivery.

Hope is a bridge we build from our own inner resources, the platform we stand on as we wait for an outcome or answer even though we don't know for sure what the resolution may be. Hope doesn't have a mystical power to assure that our preferred choice is the outcome.

Instead, hope takes work. It's the inner confidence that our being true to two responsibilities will serve us well, will carry us, as we navigate the situation—whatever may transpire.

Hope includes...

1. managing a situation with all the understanding that we can invest through engaged thinking and learning; and

---

Notes

2. deciphering any struggles at play, remembering them for what they are: either truths defrosting from our childhood freezer or truths cropping up like weeds from childhood that make our waiting even harder.

Hope is an equation calling for our active participation.

$$\text{Understanding the Situation} + \text{Deciphering Our Struggling}$$
$$= \text{Genuine and Gentle Hope}$$

This makes hope active, not passive. Understanding the situation means engaged thinking and learning. Deciphering our struggling—whether it's about a health issue, a marriage conflict, a financial challenge, or a hang-nail—recognizes the truth defrosting from our childhood freezer or the weed that's cropped up from childhood. As our struggling is deciphered, extra energy and agency then become available for moving forward with additional understanding—with grace and courage as well—even though the outcome is unclear.

Example 1. We so want it to snow. We look at the weather reports for the next week and see that snow is possible in five days—but not guaranteed. This is understanding the situation.

However, if we're holding our breath or metaphorically crossing our fingers as we wait for the snow to actually arrive, we are passively struggling, trying to exert a power which is not ours. We've called it hoping. But in this case, what we're calling hope is really a sense of false power. It's a leftover from childhood when we believed that, if we passively hoped enough, something we wanted to happen would indeed happen. This is passive, false power masquerading as hope. It's a remnant of the blind wishing we used many times to get us through childhood.

Hope can gently carry us through this waiting for snow if we're true to the equation of genuine hope: understanding the situation through engaged thinking and learning + deciphering the dimensions of struggle at play in the situation as well.

Example 2. We are extremely sick in the hospital. Our painful physical symptoms persist, and the medical professionals have little clarity as to what the issue is. We lay there hoping that everything gets better—and soon.

Notes

However, if we're not really concentrating on what the medical professionals are explaining, if we're slow to implement things they're encouraging us to try, we're not complying with our first responsibility in the equation of hope: understanding through engaged thinking and learning.

And if we're struggling with frustration but not doing all we can to determine what the struggling indicates—something thawing from our childhood freezer or a weed cropping up from childhood—we're not connecting the dots with whatever early life truth the heat of the medical situation has surfaced for us. Perhaps when we were a child, a parent was trying to teach us something, but we just weren't catching on and felt defeated. Or there was a time when we were especially afraid and simply zoned out to survive that experience of our childhood.

Until we connect these dots, we're not complying with our second responsibility in the equation of hope: deciphering struggle. The struggle of frustration is then holding us hostage just as much as our physical condition is. We're not engaging in our responsibilities. If we were doing so, we'd be building and standing on a bridge of gentle hope.

Example 3. Two people are employed by the same organization. At various times and for distinct reasons, each has had differences of opinion regarding decisions that have been made on their work teams.

One employee has demonstrated a disappointing pattern. After every dispute of theirs has been sorted through, they would find something new about which to be upset or feel affronted. This person would cause an endless stream of problem-solving energy to be invested in them. Although this person's pattern is clear, once we realize that our struggling with this colleague is similar to our experience with a parent—that we kept trying with them even though nothing we did or said ever seemed to be good enough for them, that our hoping for something different was never realized—we catch our breath, step back from our trying today, see the pattern as it is, and can say "Enough is enough" regarding the repetition of this game.

The other employee has also been upset about decisions at work on several occasions. However, this person has routinely been willing to listen and understand, make valid requests of management, and still stay active as a team player throughout the resolution of the issue. Collaboration with this person has been challenging for sure, but it's never become a struggle because there's confidence that our investment of time and energy with this person will

---

Notes

be beneficial. Disputes with them have routinely been settled amicably and productively. That's why there's valid reason to have hope.

So, to build our bridge of hope, we start with engaged understanding. Then we decipher any struggling at play. After deciphering any struggling, we can then redirect some of the energy being drained by struggling and use it to do more understanding of the situation. Both responsibilities—engaged understanding + deciphering struggle—will serve us well. We'll be standing on a platform of engaged self-responsibility with actions that are in our power, with actions over which we have agency, the best bridge to be on as we wait.

> *Both responsibilities*
> *—engaged understanding + deciphering struggle—*
> *will serve us well.*

However, *hope*—as we have so often used the word—can be unfair to us. We can be asking for too much from ourself, for example:

- hoping before a trip to another country that we can become fluent in that country's language within only a week,

- hoping our manager at work will one day become the warm human being we'd so wish that person to be, or

- hoping a dying parent won't die.

Because hope has been promulgated as something so wonderful, we have at times ascribed false dreams to the word *hope*. We have often lived with false hope and then found ourself caught up in an emotional virus which can be called MTT: Maybe This Time. We can live the false hope of MTT regarding a spouse, a parent, a family system, a co-worker, anyone...

- Maybe this time a certain person won't make things "all about them."

- Maybe this time someone won't shut down a suggestion because "no one's going to tell them what to do."

- Maybe this time this person won't make me feel small.

Notes

89

This is where false hope has been most operative in each of us—not about whether snow will fall—but hope that someone with whom we have some type of a relationship, someone with whom we interact, will change. Many of us have invested a lot of energy to get someone to change who isn't assuming that responsibility for themself. "If I approach the situation in just the right way, or if I find just the right words to say, they'll understand, change, and settle down my frustration with them."

The MTT (Maybe This Time) virus of false hope operative in us is almost always in response to an emotional virus unconsciously active and not being responsibly managed in someone else. Emotional viruses that we encounter in others—and sometimes in ourself—are variations of false power that are unconsciously driving *them* just as MTT may be unconsciously but actively driving *us*. Just a few examples of emotional viruses—in alphabetical order—include:

- *The AAM Virus: All About Me*

  When someone talks about no one other than themself and shows no interest in anyone else—most likely a leftover hunger from childhood for someone to be focused on them with genuine interest—and the false hope they can get that hunger from childhood satisfied now

- *The BTM Virus: Back To Me*

  A variation of the AAM Virus when, no matter what anyone may contribute to a conversation, someone will take the content of a conversation and make it about them again, because growing up no one ever genuinely made it about them—and "maybe this time" (MTT) someone will finally do so;

- *The CTS Virus: Calling The Shots*

  When "No one's going to tell me what to do" because, at some point in life, someone unjustly, inappropriately forced their will on them with demands of one kind or another—including sexual demands or intimidation—and so the false hope of power and control is at play;

- *The LT Virus: Lazy Thinking*

  What may be one of the most prevalent emotional viruses in the world, a virus that even the very intelligent and accomplished may have—laziness about thinking something through, understanding something or someone, connecting the dots—be it about self-awareness, family impacts on us, relationships,

---

Notes

social justice issues, or any topic—the false hope that an individual doesn't have to be responsibly engaged using their mind and heart throughout life;

- *The MTT Virus: Maybe This Time*

  As already noted, what takes hold of an individual up against any of these other emotional viruses;

- *The PLM Virus: Please Like Me*

  When someone's unmet childhood needs to feel liked, valued, and appreciated are influencing much of what they do in life, how they do it, how they present themself—all with the false hope that feeling liked, valued, and appreciated today can make up for what didn't happen in childhood;

- *The TOM-TOM Virus: Think Of Me-Think Of Me*
  (and its variation, LAM-LAM: Look At Me-Look At Me)

  When everything said or done by someone is to ensure they stay present with us—on our mind, in our heart, "under our skin"—even though this is often accomplished through annoying, frustrating, or hurting us;

- *The UYS Virus: Under Your Skin*

  When someone loves to get a reaction from you, a desperate way for them to get close to you and have you engage with them—even though it's done in a counterproductive way—another leftover hunger from a critical childhood need not met by a parent: the need to feel close and connected;

- *The W5 Virus: I Want What I Want When I Want It*

  A variation of the CTS Virus which is ramped up through pressure and urgency; and

- *The YNW Virus: You'll Never Win*

  Another variation of the CTS Virus, in this case demonstrated when nothing you say, how you say it, what you try, or how kind you are is allowed by another person to make any difference—so that you feel what they once felt.

And we will each find our own words to describe other emotional viruses that we identify in ourself or in others.

Notes

Whether MTT or any other emotional virus, these viruses are residue from a person's early life. We'll experience them being active in relationships and sometimes for generations throughout a family system. We'll even see these unconscious emotional viruses active in leaders of countries, for example the viruses of AAM (All About Me), CTS (Calling The Shots), LT (Lazy Thinking), and TOM-TOM (Think Of Me-Think of Me).

These unconscious emotional viruses have most likely been active off-and-on forever as part of someone's strategy for navigating a parent or their family of origin, a way to claim some sense of self, value, dignity, connection, or personal power. Sometimes the virus was/is a way to emulate a parent or family member, perhaps the only way found to have some sort of connection with them.

So, someone can be blind to the virus at work in them if it helped them claim an existence, a presence for themself in the world, or if it bonded them to a parent, their family members, or their family system. If a particular emotional virus operative in someone else was also a part of our own family system, it can sting us with an extra strength when it impacts us.

> *If a particular virus operative in someone else*
> *was also part of our own family system,*
> *it can sting us with an extra strength when it impacts us.*

When any of these emotional viruses are not managed effectively, they take over a person's thinking and behavior. The person with the active virus "infects" others, draining energy from them. If we're the one being impacted, MTT can then take us over. Our desperate wishing—false hoping—ramps up for these viruses active in someone else to go away, shift course, become inactive.

When we're the one with the emotional virus—MTT or any other—our responsible self-awareness is our best way to manage it. When realizing that we've been unconsciously driven by MTT when interacting with an individual or with a human system (family, friendship group, work team) that's infected with any form of an emotional virus, it's important to be honest that this has been a misplacement of our energy. This is a self-respecting and fair acknowledgment, not any reason to be harsh with ourself about having been caught up in MTT.

Notes

However, when it's someone else with an emotional virus, we can "hope and hope" that someone making us feel a certain way can change, or that we can find the right words to say, or that we can do something to make a difference. But if a person or a family has no conscious awareness of the pain caused by their emotional virus as it's inflicted on others—nor the desire to know about and manage it—then the virus is running them and wearying us.

In each case, we can be responsible in a unique way and keep MTT from overtaking us yet again. Perhaps we can apply a variation of the public health guidelines that had been recommended throughout the pandemic of the COVID-19 virus. Perhaps we can:

Wear a mask (metaphorically) if we encounter someone with an active emotional virus. This does not mean being fake with that person, and it could go against a value that suggests we should always be our authentic, transparent self. In some cases, we simply can't be our fully honest and disclosing self because it won't be valued. Maintaining respectful protection for our authentic self is truly important.

For example, the people with whom we can be our authentic self are those whom we have on the Gold Plan of our self-giving in life, those to whom we give our absolute best and most generous self, those who value who we are and what we have to offer.

Others may be on the Silver or Bronze Plans. Still others may be on the least generous giving plan, a giving plan that includes human respect, of course, but less generosity of spirit and self because what we'd be giving would be dismissed. Therefore, some people and situations might only be on the Aluminum or even the Cardboard Plan.

This is the exact intention of the harshly worded phrase, "Don't throw your pearls at swine." This is not to call anyone swine, but it dramatically recommends that we don't give something of value to anyone who would squander it. We don't give an expensive crystal vase to a two-year-old as a toy. We can maintain kindness and civility to certain others without being extra warm and investing of ourself. However, the purpose of sharing something of value whether from one's character or from one's possessions is that it gets shared further.

So, when we can't—and really shouldn't—be our authentic self, we can and should wear a mask.

Notes

Social distance. When our hope regarding others is false hope—perhaps hoping that someone will show genuine interest in us and be free to some degree of the AAM or any other emotional virus—it's important that we claim some protection from the hurt and energy drain that false hope can cause.

We may have to place some limit on the number of encounters we have with a person or situation. We may lessen the duration of an interaction, for example, staying at a social gathering for ninety minutes rather than for three hours. It's whatever degree of social distancing will be helpful for us while at the same time maintaining a level of respect for the person or situation at hand.

Wash (massage) your hands. Navigating interpersonal situations can be difficult and delicate work. So, when an individual or group is indeed hard work for you, literally wash your hands—or care for your hands in some gentle way—afterward. This doesn't have to be done in a harsh way (although the encounter may have indeed been a rough one) such that "we're washing our hands of them." It's simply a gesture for gently re-anchoring ourself with ourself after some hard emotional work.

Even when we would wash our hands after grocery shopping in the earliest days of the COVID pandemic, what we were doing was more than washing off any traces of a virus. We were re-anchoring ourself in ourself, giving ourself a sense that we were home and that we were safe.

It might be that we literally wash our hands with soap and warm water. Perhaps we take a few moments to gently massage in some hand cream. We know how soothing and even energy replenishing it can be to do so when our hands are dry as they often are after washing dishes or in wintry weather. This ten or fifteen seconds can quiet us.

So, whether it's with soap and water, hand sanitizer, hand cream, or through a dry massaging of our hands, it's important that we're soothing to ourself after doing hard emotional work, work from which we are now stepping back and catching our breath. Washing, massaging our hands: a physical way to re-anchor ourself in ourself after the hard work of navigating our own or someone else's emotional virus.

Wear a mask. Social distance. Wash (massage) your hands.

Notes

We have all lived with more false hope—more MTT—than we've imagined. If we invest our skills to manage the current situation through understanding, if we remember that any struggle regarding the situation is something from childhood that's either defrosting or cropping up like a choking weed because of the situation we're navigating, then we'll be standing on a bridge of genuine, gentle hope constructed from our own active inner resources. We will be anchored in ourself while waiting for an outcome that so concerns us—no matter what that outcome might be.

We'll realize that there are times when *hope* isn't the right word at all because our engaged understanding and deciphered struggling may tell us otherwise. We may find that a phrase like *cautious waiting* may be more universally fair to use.

Dare It Be Said: Love

The word *love* is used to identify how personally and intimately someone connects with us or to describe what we receive from another person. We often say that someone loves me because of all they do for me, how kind they are to me, how much I enjoy being with the person. When it comes to the relationship between parent and child, love is routinely characterized by the sacrifices a parent makes to assure their child is housed, clothed, fed, physically/medically healthy, educated, and supported in extra-curricular and career interests.

Seldom does someone use the most important criterion to determine if there is love between two people: the criterion of being *known*. This is what most determines love. People can be kind to us, caring, responsible, even selfless. All these forms of personal connection are to be valued and appreciated.

However, if someone does seemingly positive things for me—even at great sacrifice to themself—but doesn't know me, makes no effort to know me, that is, to know how I think and why, how I feel and why, what I value and why, what hurts me and why, then that's not really love. Someone may be doing good and being kind, but it's not truly love.

It's so difficult for people to ask the question about whether they genuinely felt loved by a parent when there may be much evidence of all the parent has generously done for them. However, if a parent never expressed interest in knowing their child, in trying to know them as the person they are, then the child was cared for responsibly and possibly quite generously by their parent, but not loved—as hard as this may be to know.

Notes

It's not possible to genuinely love someone without engaging in knowing them. It's not possible to genuinely feel loved if one doesn't feel known by the person doing the loving.

> *It's not possible to genuinely feel loved*
> *if one doesn't feel known by the person doing the loving.*

Some Non-Four-Letter Words and Phrases

Depression

Depression is a word that makes someone feel worse. It's like one of those big industrial augers that we've seen used at commercial building sites, those huge corkscrews that drill into the ground. When the words depression or depressed are used, it's like we or someone else straps us to one of those industrial augers. Each time either word is used we're drilled down even more. It would be much more helpful if we did two things.

First, listen to the word itself. To be de-pressed is to be *pressed down*. That's what we do with certain levers and with the gas pedal in a car. We de-press it. We press it down.

If we're being pressed down by pressures at work, by the responsibilities of childcare or elder care, by concerns of one kind or another, we often say we're feeling depressed. When the heat or warmth of current-day experiences such as these flash thaws frozen childhood pain, the combination of something today plus something old is a lot of emotional weight pressing us down—and that's what's really going on when the words depression or depressed have been used.

When we say we're *depressed*, the word paralyzes us. It locks us in and takes away almost all—sometimes absolutely all—the energy of our own agency. Depressed tends to bury us under the combined weight of current-day and early-life issues. The word leads many helping professionals to prescribe medication which releases nothing from us but instead packs the pain in even more tightly.

Notes

Saying *pressed down*, however, leaves room for us to navigate, to lift off from ourself—through our disciplined awareness—whatever is weighing us down. Our focus can be productive if we're lifting elements of what's weighing us down—from today, from our childhood emotional freezers, from among the weeds planted in childhood—up and off of ourself over time.

We may get these feelings up and out through the first two forms of communication: conscious, intentional efforts to write it out or talk it out. However, if we or someone else notices we're using the third form of communication—acting it out—our awareness is what will catch that this is happening, and then we decipher/decode/interpret the early life story being expressed through the acting out. Our system is going Number 3, releasing additional emotional toxins that have been stored within us, weighing us down, pressing us down, for a long, long time.

Second, a better word to use than *depressed* is the word *depleted*. The heavy loads of the present, the future, and the accumulated layers of frozen, baffling, painful experiences from our earliest days—combined with the hard work of pulling our emotional weeds from childhood each time they crop up—can leave us spent, weary, and depleted. Again, the word depressed robs us of agency. Saying we're depleted gives us context for what we might do to refill our tank, catch our breath, rest, renew our energy, and start up again.

> *Saying we're depleted gives us context for what we might do to refill out tank, catch our breath, rest, renew our energy, and start up again.*

The word depressed, by contrast, decks us. It leaves us feeling powerless and overwhelmed.

There are chemical changes in our brain when we are emotionally depleted for sure, but that doesn't necessarily mean that medication is required to adjust the chemical change. For example, we don't use medication to adjust the chemical changes that take place when we're sad and then cry. We don't look for prescription remedies to forever dry up our tears. When hair color changes as a chemical reaction to emotional stress, we'll use dye products, not medication.

Notes

To repeat something noted in the "Opening Letter to You," the questions being raised about the helpfulness of psychotropic or emotion-focused medications are by no means to imply that, if someone is using such medications, they should stop using them or can stop using them cold turkey. Any shift off even one of these medications has to be accomplished under the supervision of a medical or psychiatric professional. These medications are that powerful—even those which have come to be in such wide use and seem so commonplace.

So, if we let ourself think of the words depression and depressed as meaning pressed down, or perhaps use the word *depleted* in place of the words *depression/depressed*, we'd be *down* for a much shorter period and we'd experience how our own agency can engage and replenish us.

Just as the word *need* unconsciously puts us into a desperate life-and-death mode of thinking and feeling, the words *depression/depressed* deck us. It's just not beneficial to use these words.

> *Just as the word <u>need</u> unconsciously puts us into a desperate life-and-death mode of thinking and feeling, the words <u>depression/depressed</u> deck us. It's just not beneficial to use these words.*

Anxiety

We often hear people make statements like "I have anxiety," or "I feel so anxious." When the words *anxiety* or *anxious* are either thought or spoken, each word can feel huge, overwhelming (like the word *need*). We can feel like we're churning inside, living in a prison that leaves us alternating between feeling the red of fear and the dark of hopelessness. We feel helpless and find ourselves struggling. And all these words are completely accurate.

While *depression* is an indicator of struggle that's pressing us down and depleting us, *anxiety* is an indicator of struggle that's churning us up and panicking us. We are feeling unsettled almost beyond words, and the unsettledness leaves us feeling afraid. In either case, something has defrosted from within—or a weed from childhood has cropped up—and is asking for our attention in an agitated way.

Notes

> *While <u>depression</u> is an indicator of struggle*
> *that's pressing us down and depleting us,*
> *<u>anxiety</u> is an indicator of struggle*
> *that's churning us up and panicking us.*

When we feel unsettled to the point that the words *anxiety* or *anxious* come to mind for describing how we're feeling, it would be helpful to instead use simpler words, maybe even a word closer to one a child would use to describe such feelings. Simpler words would be *unsettled* and the child's word *afraid*.

> *Simpler words would be <u>unsettled</u> and the child's word <u>afraid</u>.*

We may be afraid about an upcoming doctor's appointment or about seeing someone who's difficult for us to be with whether within the family or at work. "I'm afraid" may itself be scary to say, but it's really a gentler use of words because the phrase doesn't take us hostage, doesn't paralyze us. We maintain room to think. We can use our agency to position ourselves for and to navigate the situation. It will help us connect the childhood feelings contributing to the swirling of the struggle, feelings from childhood of being unsettled, in turmoil, or afraid that are adding to our feeling so unsettled, in turmoil, or afraid now.

The word *anxiety* takes us prisoner almost immediately. It blocks the flow of our agency, our ability to assess, think, plan, and execute. Some people even come to unconsciously depend on the word to give a reason for why they're not being responsible for themself in whatever way. Anxiety can become a jail in which we get to be busy with churning and not really doing anything substantive, and yet we can get lots of concern from others during our stay in that jail.

Depression can be such a jail, too, that gets us lots of concern from others.

Saying that we're unsettled or afraid rather than anxious or having anxiety will help us both articulate whatever may be going on today and also identify the simultaneously thawed-out moments of fear from childhood—or the weeds of fear planted in childhood—that are active again now. By articulating what's now and identifying what's old, we sustain our agency.

Notes

Let It Go / Get Over It

Let it go is asking someone to have a false hope that it's possible to ignore or push away certain thoughts and feelings. It implies something metaphorically floating away. *Get over it* is an unfair expectation to put on ourself or on anyone else.

What we can do when something impacts us in a significant and overly painful way is to chip away at understanding it, identify its impact on us, and find the childhood root that's been inflamed and is leaving us in a place of struggle.

We can let out more and more. We can release more from within us in order to hold it before us, to see it, and to study it more effectively. And then we can set it down rather than let it go.

In fact, we don't want to let it go because we have just come to know and understand additional moments from our autobiography, something it's time to face, something that's part of the story of our life's journey. We're not honoring the painful things that happened to us when we were children. However, we are giving honor and respect to ourself or to someone else for having endured and navigated those baffling, painful situations—not as adults—but as children. We grieve what happened to us as children, and the grieving will continue to varying degrees forever.

We would never tell one of the parents who tragically lost their beloved child at Sandy Hook Elementary in 2012—or ever expect them—to let it go or get over it. We can't get over it on a personal level any more than the world can let go of or get over World War II, the COVID-19 pandemic, or our collective witnessing of the 2022 invasion of Ukraine. Nor can the United States let go of or get over the racial injustices of lynching and burning. These are all examples of loss and death.

For a child, the bafflements of hurt, fear, confusion, or any other whiplashing, traumatic experience of a parent or other family member are moments of loss, the loss of trust and security. They are moments of death, the death of what every child presumed would be their safe experience of themself and of life because of the person(s) who invited them into the world, into their life, and into their home.

Is there effort involved with letting out, releasing, looking at, studying, understanding, and knowing moments of our life that have been stored within us, perhaps for decades? Yes, there is. It calls for an investment of time and energy.

Notes

However, *let it go* and *get over it* are unfair demands that we place on ourself. They are also unjust expectations suggested to us by those unable or afraid to support us through our process, by those who think they should do something to help but can't do anything, and so impose on us the responsibility of getting rid of the troubling reality at hand that is so uncomfortable for them—let alone for us.

> **Let it go and get over it are unfair demands that we place on ourself.**
> **They are also unjust expectations suggested to us by others.**

We can't let go of the flare-ups—the defrosted moments from our childhood emotional freezer or the reappearance of early life weeds—that will happen throughout our life. Every time they become present, we simply have to own them with our awareness, and then set them down—possibly literally so—through writing them on paper.

Accept and Embrace

When it comes to current-day pain or long-stored frozen childhood pain, pain is pain. There is nothing to *accept* about pain. There is nothing to *embrace* about pain, nothing to feel warm and good and cuddled-up with when it comes to pain. Can having a connection with pain be an unconsciously misguided connection with those who caused the pain, for example, a connection to a parent? Yes, it can be.

We can navigate pain—whether it's physical or emotional—and learn ways to manage it. We can learn about it and learn from it. However, when we find ourself not being able to accept or embrace our physical or emotional pain, we end up being more discouraged, disappointed in and hard on ourself, and we lose the energy required to learn about and learn from it, to navigate and manage it.

It's worth it to use our energies in the most productive and effective of ways. Putting expectations of accepting or embracing pain on ourself or others is neither productive nor effective for us to do.

> **Putting expectations of accepting or embracing pain on ourself**
> **or others is neither productive nor effective for us to do.**

Notes

Forgiveness

Forgiveness is an expectation we place on ourself, or an expectation placed on us by someone else. The presumption is that forgiveness should be somewhat easy to do. When we can't forgive, we often feel badly about ourself for not being able to do so. The presumption isn't fair, and berating ourself regarding it isn't fair either.

Although we talk about forgiveness between individuals, we often associate it with a clergyperson offering forgiveness. It's indeed easy for a clergyperson to forgive someone and send the person on their way because, very likely, nothing about the person asking forgiveness was a personal burden or affront to the clergyperson in the first place. True forgiveness is not this image of clergyperson and penitent. It's not that simple. True forgiveness is this: offering understanding to the offending person and then extending to both that person and oneself the invitation to move forward.

> *True forgiveness is this:*
> *Offering understanding to the offending person*
> *and then extending to both that person and oneself*
> *the invitation to move forward.*

Forgiveness without understanding is not true forgiveness. That's why we haven't been able to forgive at times. Unconsciously, we've known that forgiveness is not moving forward with eyes closed. We've instinctively known that moving forward in a genuine way includes at least some degree of eyes-open, conscious understanding. Understanding is what's most called for and the most critical component within the concept of forgiveness. However, understanding takes time and effort. Over time it leads to compassion both for others and for ourself.

Within the Christian tradition, there is a noteworthy example in the Bible's New Testament that suggests that a shift in our understanding of forgiveness is warranted.

Christians have often heard during Good Friday services that Christ forgave his crucifiers, that he was somehow able to set aside his negative feelings for the people who had tortured and crucified him. The teaching around this story has implied to the listener that, if you can't forgive as Christ forgave, it certainly speaks to a character flaw in you.

Notes

Instead, as the New Testament recounts the details of that event, Christ never said that he forgave his crucifiers. The Gospel of Luke talks about his prayer, his talking to his Father in heaven about what had happened to him, and recounts Christ saying this:

> *"Father, forgive them, for they do not know what they are doing."*
> *(Luke 23:34)*

Christ demonstrated understanding—his crucifiers didn't know what they were doing—but he didn't forgive them. He asked his Father to do so.

Another example which refers the act of forgiveness to someone other than ourself, and in which the speaker demonstrates understanding, not forgiveness, is this writing by an Islamic scholar:

> *I saw the Messenger of Allah, peace and blessings be upon him,*
> *tell the story of a prophet who was beaten by his people*
> *and he wiped the blood from his face, saying:*
> *"My Lord, forgive my people for they do not know."*
> *(Sahih Bukhari 6530)*

The Quran addresses pardon/forgiveness in a similar way:

> *"You shall resort to pardon, advocate tolerance, and disregard the ignorant."*
> *(The Quran 7:199)*

Perhaps this quote is also indicating that the real emphasis within the concept of forgiveness should be understanding. Tolerance is a dimension of understanding. Attributing ignorance to someone and their actions is also a type of understanding because it provides a context for why the wrong action possibly took place.

At one point in the New Testament's Gospel of Matthew, Christ is asked how many times someone should forgive someone else. The questioner asked, "Seven times?"

Christ answered:

> *"Not seven times. Seventy times seven times."*
> *(Matthew 18:22)*

Notes

This passage is routinely presented as encouragement for endless forgiveness. Or might the message in this example really be "Forgive as many times as you want. Understanding is much more important."

Another Islamic scholar has addressed this same topic, the number of times one should forgive. Perhaps it's worth considering a similar reinterpretation of this verse:

"O Messenger of Allah, how many times should I pardon my servant?"
The Messenger of Allah, peace and blessings be upon him, said:
"Seventy times in each day."
(Sunan At-Tirmidhi 1949)

The New Testament has additional examples of Christ understanding the plight and suffering of someone, examples of understanding rather than of forgiveness. Based on understanding, he extended the invitation to Mary Magdalene and so many others to move forward together.

In the Hebrew Bible—the foundation for Christ's own religious formation—Psalm 25, verses 16-20, supports the idea that understanding a person is what gives substance to forgiveness:

"Look upon me, have pity on me, for I am alone and afflicted.
Relieve the troubles of my heart, bring me out of my distress.
Look upon my affliction and suffering, take away all my sins.
See how many are my enemies. See how fiercely they hate me.
Preserve my soul and rescue me.
Do not let me be disgraced, for in you I seek refuge."

This segment from Psalm 25 is all about understanding someone's plight as the important dimension of the forgiveness being sought, of the request to "take away all my sins."

Let's not keep the word forgiveness as an unfair and heavy burden on our shoulders whether we or someone else has put it there. It's even insulting to the ultimate beauty and power of the word to use it prematurely or flippantly. Let's start instead with what is appropriate and possible to do over time: understanding whatever the painful story was that someone was acting out of themselves even though it might have been at our

---

Notes

expense. This is also true when the issue is about forgiving oneself for something that we may have been acting out.

It will take time to walk the path of understanding. However, after whatever length of time that walk might take, we will have given to another—or to ourself—the best of gifts: understanding. If forgiveness is to have a place, it will arrive all on its own if we have first been true to the hard work of understanding.

> *If forgiveness is to have a place, it will arrive all on its own*
> *if we have first been true to the hard work of understanding.*

Guilt

Guilt is something assigned to us by ourself or by someone else when it's been determined we were not acting responsibly and have therefore caused harm to someone or something. This is what the guilty verdict is in a court of law.

We express our guilt, our sense of not being accountable, of being irresponsible, when we admit our contribution to what was wrongly done or not done, said or not said, for how it was done or said, and for the resulting negative impact on a person or situation. This is admitting guilt in an appropriate way. Any punishment assigned to us as a result is a way to make us symbolically pay—be accountable—for the wrong we did.

However, far too often we use guilt in our own minds and hearts in a different way. We self-guilt as a protective diversion from something that hurts us so much that we don't know what to do with it. We unconsciously park on ourself what so disappoints us in someone else, or perhaps put on ourself the responsibility for an awful hurt someone caused us. We do so out of desperation, not knowing where else to put the disappointment or hurt.

Such self-guilt has been especially common among those who have tragically experienced sexual assault: "What did I do wrong? What messages did I give that provoked the assault?" But it's the perpetrator who did the terrible, disgusting wrong.

Again, when someone disappoints us, hurts us, or even disgusts us, we don't know what to do about their behavior. This is especially true when we are children and the person disillusioning us is a parent or someone else within our family. So, we self-guilt to feel

---

Notes

guilty because we get something seemingly positive out of feeling guilty. We get hope, but it's false hope. How do we get hope out of self-guilting? Here's an example.

Example. When we were in the fifth grade, we made the commitment to be home in time after school to babysit a younger sibling, but we didn't fulfill our commitment. By not fulfilling this responsibility, we were putting our sibling in danger. Corrective, direct, and strong feedback to us from our parent was both appropriate and genuinely important. We had to own our irresponsibility, learn from it, and demonstrate how seriously we will approach such commitments in the future.

However, when giving us their corrective feedback, our parent talked to us in such a way that made us feel like we were not only at fault, but that we were worth nothing, saying things to us like, "How could you be so stupid? Where is your brain?" Being strong in feedback was called for, but our parent was being harsh.

If, in response to this corrective feedback, we became more focused on our feeling stupid and on chastising ourself harshly rather than on being resolute regarding our responsibilities going forward, we were then doing to ourself what was just inappropriately done to us. We were being harsh to ourself, excessively devaluing ourself—self-guilting—but the harsh one was, in fact, the parent who talked to us in such a disparaging way.

Our irresponsibility was wrong, but our parent's words were too much—even if their intent was to communicate how seriously wrong we had been. Our parent's words were disappointing, devaluing, and hurtful. Their strength may have even been terrifying for the child we were. Whether consciously or not, we were afraid to be honest with ourself, let alone with our parent, about the impact on us of those harsh words. We didn't know what to do.

So, we did the only thing we could do with those overly harsh words: we parked them on ourself. We shifted from rightly owning our irresponsibility, from being focused in a new way on our behavior going forward, to feeling guilty. The focus on a new commitment to responsibility was there, but it was there to a much lesser degree than our reaction to the experience of our parent going too far in how they made us feel.

There was indeed a problem with our irresponsible behavior in this example. We had both the responsibility and the personal power to monitor and manage our behavior going forward.

Notes

However, when a parent's behavior is inappropriate, when important teaching and coaching becomes a personal assault against their child, that child—because they are only a child—has no real power to execute a change in their parent's behavior. But if the child adopts the hurtful, disparaging behavior of the parent as an approach to themself, they have the chance for a substitute victory even though it will be a false one. If the child becomes responsible for both parts of the wrong behavior—theirs and their parent's—two things can be accomplished:

1. The child can pretend that how their parent treated them wasn't that bad, didn't impact them as strongly as it did, and didn't hurt as much as it did.

2. The child can work toward a false victory by fixing in themself those things they can do nothing about in their parent.

This self-guilting is what we most often call feeling guilty and what leads us to be unjustly harsh with ourself. In self-guilt we have found the perfect diversion for the terrible pain caused by another person. Through self-guilt, we have found a world of false hope and false power in which to live. Self-guilt makes us the problem when we're not the problem. It diverts to us—unfairly and falsely so—what so pains us about someone or something else.

> *Self-guilt makes us the problem when we're not the problem.*
> *It diverts to us—unfairly and falsely so—*
> *what so pains us about someone or something else.*

Again, we first used self-guilt in this way when we were children because any disappointing, hurtful, frightening, and even disgusting disregard and treatment of us by a parent or other family member was too much for us to bear. However, if we thought of ourself as the one who wasn't doing something right, wasn't doing their job, we then lived with the false hope and false power that we could fix it, whatever "it" might have been.

Self-guilt lets us get busy when we feel powerless. Self-guilt becomes our safe place, a safe place against great pain.

> *Self-guilt lets us get busy when we feel powerless.*
> *Self-guilt becomes our safe place, a safe place against great pain.*

Notes

Closure

As much as we may wish for it, there is no *closure* when there's been a significant emotional hurt. Greater understanding is possible, but such understanding unfolds over time as our system's way of being kind to us. Our emotional system lets us move gently into the place of fuller understanding.

Each of us would, of course, want to feel less burdened, less sad, or less disgusted. However, the nature of emotional pain is such that there is no closure, simply better places of understanding and quieting peace at which we can arrive over time.

> *The nature of emotional pain is such that there is no closure, simply better places of understanding and quieting peace at which we can arrive over time.*

Happy Birthday

There are some among us—very few, unfortunately, if we are going to be honest—who felt truly welcomed into the world and completely safe on the day of their birth. For those who felt genuinely welcomed, wishing them *"Happy Birthday"* is totally appropriate.

However, we don't exactly know who these truly welcomed people are. We don't know how safe someone viscerally felt on the day of their birth. We don't know those for whom "Happy Birthday" would be a completely appropriate wish.

Anecdotal evidence about how a baby responds in the womb, from within their room in the *Parent Hotel*, indicates that a baby reacts with pleasure to calming music or a gentle massaging of the carrying parent's stomach. A baby is negatively impacted by improper substance use by a parent. Twins play outside the womb in ways that resemble what their play was like within the womb, for example, standing on either side of sheer curtains trying to poke and tickle each other.

It's clear that a baby in the womb is a developing person already taking in everything—literally everything—that's going on outside the walls of their room in the Parent Hotel.

Notes

Someone's time in the womb may have been marked by great sadness because of:

- the death of a parent before the child's birth;

- something with which the carrying parent may have been struggling, like the death of one of their own parents or a separation from their life partner during pregnancy;

- a house fire during pregnancy that the family survived;

- how two parents talked with and interacted with each other—or didn't; or

- whether a parent was only tolerating the arrival of their child rather than truly anticipating with authentic joy the day of their child's birth.

These are only a few examples of what someone may have sensed going on outside their room in the Parent Hotel.

> *The baby is a developing person already taking in everything*
> *—literally everything—*
> *going on outside the walls of their room in the Parent Hotel.*

Depending on what we were being born into, the actual day of our birth may have been wonderful. However, it also might have been the day when what was already confusing or alarming us while inside the womb was now ours to actually navigate. It might have been the day when our first experience of being alive was to be given away if we were put up for adoption.

In some Asian cultures, the day of a birth, a birthday, is called "Mother Danger Day." Although in prior times there was more danger for both the person giving birth and for the person being born, giving birth still poses a risk for both.

The day of our birth may not have been a happy one for us—an unconscious awareness, but an accurate one.

Then, if during our early life, a parent didn't acknowledge our birthday with interest and joy, birthdays were likely days with a lot of sadness whether we remember feeling

Notes

that sadness or not. We might have been afraid to feel the sadness that such a disappointment by a parent caused us.

There are a variety of reasons why someone may not like their birthday. Even if a person anticipates the arrival of their next birthday with seeming excitement, the day itself may not be experienced as the good day they had been expecting it to be. Sometimes the days leading up to their birthday can be somewhat heavy and dark because of the visceral memory of those last days in the relative safety of the Parent Hotel.

We may feel so very good about someone such that the anniversary of their birth means the world to us. But to the person whose birthday it is, unconsciously it may not be the most happy or peaceful of days. Sending someone "Good Wishes on the Anniversary of Your Birth" may be kinder than saying "Happy Birthday," and it would always be appropriate.

Please note: While there is much evidence that a baby is indeed an emotional being while in the womb, the exact moment when a baby's emotional self comes to life is not known. This acknowledgment by no means implies any disregard of life decisions that someone carrying a baby has to make for themself and for their baby.

Some of these decisions are torturous ones, and the right to these decisions belongs to each pregnant person. Rescinding a person's right to such choices, per the overturning of *Roe v. Wade* in the United States in June 2022, is an egregious assault on the unique dignity of the relationship between a carrying parent and their child.

Concluding Thoughts on "Bad" Words

"Bad" words are words which can do us emotional harm, words that do injustice to us in ways we may have never consciously realized, words which take us away from truth and leave us pretending. And the promise we each want to make to ourself is *telling the truth and no more pretending.*

Notes

9. The Kaleidoscope of Three-Dimensional Living

Well-intended invitations and encouragements like *being present* and *living in the moment* put unfair expectations on people because these concepts imply someone is less than disciplined, practiced, or evolved when their being present or living in the moment is hard to achieve. The gentleness that being present and living in the moment is intended to provide for someone often ends up burdening and discouraging them.

When someone finds it difficult to be present, to live in the moment, they wonder what might be wrong with them. They wonder what they're not doing right. On the other hand, perhaps their entire system—physical, mental, and emotional—is telling them that there's something not quite right about the goal.

Is there something good about being present and living in the moment? Absolutely. However, it's not good if either is thought to be *the* indicator of maturity and self-management. Taking both phrases as being equal, if doing either—being present or living in the moment—is an end in itself, we disrespect ourself by forgetting the reality of what it means to be human, the reality that we are each a *three-dimensional person*.

Every moment is an ever-shifting, dynamic kaleidoscope of:

- managing, navigating, and enjoying the ***PRESENT***,

- looking to, envisioning, and building the ***FUTURE***, and

- recognizing, decoding, and understanding the difficult truths of our earliest ***PAST***, all that's been stored in our childhood emotional freezers, all the weeds that had been planted in us, the truth of what it was like for us to be a child. Good truth from our early life doesn't call for additional work on our part now because it didn't cause us to store any hurt or bafflement.

So, being present or living in the moment is, in fact, the ability to live in the three-dimensional kaleidoscope of being human that every moment is. Neither being present nor living in the moment is possible if it means a focus on just one dimension of life.

Notes

> *Living in the moment is, in fact, the ability to live in the three-dimensional kaleidoscope of being human that every moment is.*

Example. We are communicating with a friend via voice or text. We want to be tuned in to them by being fair and respectful, by taking them seriously—the ways we express that they are worth our time and attentiveness. As the two of us are communicating, we become simultaneously aware that we have to be on our way somewhere in ten minutes. And then something comes up in the conversation that reminds the two of us about something we shared together on a vacation eight years ago.

This example illustrates the dynamic reality that we are three-dimensional people, that being human is an ever-active, ever-shifting, three-dimensional experience, a truth so worth staying aware of, practicing, and living. The invitation to manage this natural kaleidoscope of being human is a much fairer goal and invitation to ourself and to others than is the implication that living in the moment—when it equals only the present—is the most desired goal.

Therefore, to live our life as effectively as possible, a beneficial and rich daily promise to ourself is to stay aware of and limber regarding what it means to live in the moment—with "the moment" defined as the ever-shifting, three-dimensional experience of:

- managing, navigating, and enjoying the ***PRESENT***,

- looking to, envisioning, and building the ***FUTURE***, and

- recognizing, decoding, and understanding our baffling and hurtful ***PAST***, our oldest past, whatever's been in storage in our childhood emotional freezer, whichever weeds persist since then, the difficult truths of what it was like for each of us to be a child.

The lack of awareness of our childhood history denies us access to ownership of our complete autobiography, denies us living a three-dimensional life as a three-dimensional person. Even in counseling for life partners, rather than having a three-dimensional focus, the counseling's focus is often only the two-dimensions of:

Notes

- interactions in the present (for example, communication), and
- envisioning and planning the future (for example, where life partners see themselves in five years and beyond).

Every struggle is an invitation for a person to own a part of their early life autobiography, an opportunity to look at a thawed moment or a weed cropped up from childhood that's piggybacking on a current-day event. When we invest some time looking at this, we quiet the piggybacker and return to better footing for the issue of the day.

This same dynamic is important for life partners to understand and integrate into their shared life. That's why so often life partners sense that an argument they might be having is not really about whatever the topic of their disagreement appears to be. And they're right.

When logic isn't getting an individual or life partners anywhere beyond the struggle they're experiencing, their distress is the flash thawing of a frozen moment from one person's childhood freezer—and sometimes from the freezer of each person simultaneously. The distress is coming from the third dimension of being human that's routinely not remembered and considered: from a person's baffling and hurtful past, from their childhood emotional freezer, from among the weeds of false belief about themselves, the world, and life that had been planted in them long ago.

Remembering this dynamic is how we read the hidden, unread portions of our autobiography. Awareness of this dynamic is also what brings understanding about how a life partner or good friend may unconsciously be sharing their life story with us—and vice versa.

We are three-dimensional persons, and so, as individuals, we each do much better when we live as the three-dimensional people we are. Life partners also do better and grow in intimacy when they are aware of the three-dimensional life they share. Siblings and friends do better, too. It's really a very rich and respectful way to live with self and with others. When you think about it, would you really want to live any other way?

We do much better when we live
as the three-dimensional people that we are.
When you think about it, would you really want to live any other way?

Notes

10. A Mission of Loyalty

Struggles in life indicate the ongoing impact of stories from childhood whether they were a one-time or a recurring event. You would think that almost everyone who finds themself struggling would have the will and the interest to live ever more free from their struggles over time. A lack of such will and interest may be from the fear someone might have about living in any way other than the life of struggle they know. For others, it may be a type of emotional laziness regarding doing the work that would bring greater personal freedom.

However, even these two possibilities are part of a broader theme: the theme of loyalty to parents and family that we each unconsciously maintain in different ways and to varying degrees. Many people have become well practiced at feeling about themself and about life in the very ways they were given to feel about themself and life by how a parent and family members regarded and treated them. This set of beliefs is a connection with a parent and family members, and some people don't want to break any of these connections.

Emotional laziness may be a type of coziness with someone's emotionally lazy parents and with the family's emotionally lazy dynamics. These dynamics weren't a pleasant home in which to live, but they nevertheless were the place called home. In this context, emotional laziness is really fear because some people are simply terrified to be homeless, regardless of what that home was like, regardless of how they were treated and made to feel in that home.

If a parent consciously or unconsciously gave us reason to...

- be afraid,
- not feel good about or confident in ourself,
- be embarrassed or ashamed of ourself, or
- feel sad...

...then we may want to remain loyal to this experience of life and package of emotions that we received from a parent and our family members, staying loyal to what they told us about ourself, about the world, and about life.

Notes

When as children we are regarded and treated with disrespect, a lack of gentleness, without fairness, without a genuine feeling that we are liked, a false belief takes hold that this is all we deserve in life, that this is all we are worth. Living in compliance with any of these messages as we proceed through life is a type of dutiful loyalty to messages received about ourself. It's indeed true that hurtful messages may have been given, whether blatantly through words and actions, or subtly through looks, attitudes, and silences. However, the content of the message—that this is all we deserve or are worth—was never true.

Compliance with this messaging—regarding and treating ourself as a parent or family member once or routinely did—is a desperate way to have some kind of connection with them, with those where connection just never seemed to happen as we expected it would. It puts us in the same ballpark, on the same team, as our parent or family. The unconsciously strong appeal of belonging to the same team—even though the connection is the unjust messaging we received about ourself and about life—is simply that we have achieved connection.

In addition, we may be content to be held hostage by the emotions of struggle because this may be the only way we've ever found for feeling held by our parents and family. Yes, we're being held hostage by our struggling with unjust and unfair feelings, but at least we're being held.

> *Yes, we're being held hostage by our struggling*
> *with unjust and unfair feelings,*
> *but at least we're being held.*

Because being connected to a parent means more than anything to a baby and a child, it unconsciously continues to mean more than anything to us as life progresses until we consciously face this desperate loyalty:

- loyalty to what a parent and family members told us about ourself, about the world, about life, and

- loyalty to the fulfillment of our wish to be connected to and held by a parent and our family members by whatever means.

We can also demonstrate loyalty to a parent by ascribing to ourself descriptors that in truth belong to them.

Notes

Example 1. *We may think that we are—or come across to others as—an arrogant and self-consumed person. In fact, that may not be true about us at all. It's likely that a parent was the one who was arrogant and self-consumed, but we have parked our disappointing awareness about them on ourself.*

Example 2. *We unconsciously live to appear uncaring and irresponsible so that it would be us, their child (regardless of age), and not the parent who was uncaring and not responsible. This is likely one of the roots of the imposter syndrome that some people experience within themself.*

An adult who claimed the title *parent* may or may not have provided sufficiently for the physical and safety needs of their child. If they didn't provide for these needs, then the title parent was not accurately reflecting who this person said they were. Whether consciously or not, the scary thought that the parent is an imposter has entered the child's mind and heart.

However, when a parent has no interest in knowing their child, treasuring them, giving them all those most important of feelings and experiences which wouldn't cost the parent a penny, this for sure becomes an awareness for the child—consciously or not—that their parent is not who their title says they are. This unfortunately becomes a first—and usually privately held—experience of someone being an imposter.

Conscious or unconscious knowledge that a parent is an imposter—to whatever degree and as harsh as this may sound—is just too painful for a child to bear. It's too painful for most adults to consider such an awareness regarding a parent. But because this knowledge has to be put somewhere, it's put on the child themself. This starts unconsciously in many ways in early life and becomes more conscious and painful as the years proceed, that is, a person thinking of themself as an imposter and self-guilting, feeling like a bad person, as a result.

Example 1. *A child has been made to feel stupid, less than, and like a nobody by their parent. In truth the child is not stupid, less than, or a nobody. The child's innate presumption that their parent would be encouraging, affirming, and life-enriching proves to not be true. For the child—whether consciously or not—this introduces the scary idea that their parent is an "imposter." To protect themself and to hide from what they have come to realize about their parent, the child will unconsciously make themself the imposter.*

Notes

For the purpose of public image, the child may present themselves to the world as someone who is knowledgeable and confident, as someone with an active public persona. And the child may indeed have these positive qualities. However, because the child is not presenting themself in alignment with who their parent told them they were—stupid, less than, a nobody—the child feels like an imposter. Because they have to park their awareness of the "imposter" nature of their parent somewhere, they do so quietly on themself. For both these reasons—consciously or not—the child feels like an imposter.

This false belief is then maintained in secret for years. And providing cover for the parent in this regard becomes a very personal service to—and thus private connection with—the parent.

Example 2. A child may present themself as a happy, people-loving, engaged-with-life kind of person. However, inside—consciously or not—they carry a heavy load of sadness because of how their parents and family members have regarded and treated them, because of the embarrassment of finding people to generally be more difficult than enjoyable, and because of the daily wish for relief from the grind of each day.

The child unconsciously feels like an imposter because of how they present themself to the world—and works tirelessly to hide this secret, too. The child becomes an imposter in two ways: seemingly happy, but not; seemingly an imposter, but not.

Example 3. A child experiences their parent as being detached and uninterested in them. Sometimes the child also feels belittled by this parent. Consciously or not, the child knows that feeling this way doesn't match two things: their instinctive sense that they should feel safe with and treasured by their parent, and the images that grow for them over time from picture books and cartoons of what closeness and affection between parent and child look like—whether the images are of people or of animals.

The child begins to think consciously or unconsciously, "How can I be this person's child if this is how they regard and treat me, if again and again this is how they make me feel about myself and about being alive?" These thoughts become a way for the child to become the one detaching. "Let it be me who's detached."

The doubts about whether they are really their parent's child then lead them to wonder if they are adopted. Yet day after day the child is being presented to the world—and presents themself—as the parent's child. As a result, this child now has an ongoing, undercurrent,

---

Notes

false belief that they are living their life as an imposter: as their parent's child—but not really their child.

These are all examples in which the person with the title "parent" is not being who they say they are—and instead—is unconsciously being an imposter. The child finds a way to park that truth somewhere, but it's falsely parked on themself.

Being loyal to a parent is a way of protecting not only us from what we don't want to realize about a parent, but it's also a way of protecting our parent, covering for them, dismissing the fact that they didn't do what was most important for us. For a parent's sake and for our own, we will consciously or unconsciously choose to not know the truth about how we have come to feel about ourself—that it's the direct result of how a parent and family members regarded and treated us. Loyalty is a way to give cover for the ones who so disappointed us, and it also gives cover to ourself from these painful truths of our childhood.

However, loyalty may be giving cover to what someone may be most afraid of, give cover to what may be most terrifying. Loyalty may be our cover for:

- the *hate* we unconsciously felt as children for all the feelings we experienced and didn't know what to do with, hate for having had to flash freeze countless moments in our childhood emotional freezer;

- the *hate* we had for the weeds of false belief about ourself, about the world, and about life that a parent and family members were planting in us across the years of our childhood;

- the *hate* we had for having to work so hard to navigate the beginning of our life and every day since then; and

- the *hate* we've had for the hate we've had.

Maybe loyalty to whatever we negatively—and often unconsciously—experienced in childhood is keeping us protected from what we have feared the most: knowing the hate we have felt and carried. We may already feel badly to varying degrees about ourself. However, consciously recognizing the hate that we've felt and carried would leave us feeling like an absolutely terrible person—maybe the worst of persons—for hating how our parent and family members made us feel, for hating the weeds of false beliefs about ourself, the world, and life that they planted in us.

Notes

Any indiscriminate devaluing—of whatever kind and to whatever degree, physically, sexually, emotionally, consciously malicious or not—that we experienced in childhood would indeed have given us reason to feel hate, as scary as the feeling would have been for us. So, someone might consider being *not aware* as the better alternative, to not be honest with themself, because being aware of one's hate has simply been terrifying.

Being honest about any hate we've unconsciously carried does not imply that we should then direct this hate at anyone—including ourself—either verbally or through some sort of action. In fact, being honest about any hate we've had stored within will be an act of brave knowing that will help us to personally feel freer and lighter, and it will lessen the times this hate could leak out in words or actions against someone else or even against ourself.

The honoring of and honesty about our experience of parent and family are possible. Both are critical. Honesty gives us true understanding of the roots of our struggling in life, and understanding gives us agency to interpret and navigate the struggling.

The honesty will also lead us to a greater compassion for and honoring of a parent. As we apply to our parent what we apply to ourself regarding the impacts of a parent on a child, over time we will arrive at a new place of understanding about how our parent's early life shaped them, insight into how they began their own journey on the earth. We'll have a new perspective of why they kicked this can of generational trauma down the road to us: because, unfortunately, the impacts of their early life have remained unconscious to them.

This doesn't mean that knowing and understanding can substantively change our experience of a parent, but it does give us either better footing for navigating the relationship or clearer reason for staying apart from it.

With arrival at a new understanding of and compassion for a parent, a new level of honoring them can happen, but only following the unpacking, defrosting, weeding, and knowing of our own stories. This is what lets us truly own and be ourself.

As we come to believe that breaking from our mission of loyalty to a parent will not diminish any connection we have with them—there will always be a connection because we are parent and child—we will find that, in fact, we have a new fairness toward and respect for both ourself and for them.

Notes

New understandings of self and of parents will come. They always do—if we let ourself be willing and brave to do this work.

More Letters

11. To Life Partners

To Those in a Life Partner Relationship:

When individuals consider a relationship of life commitment with each other, when people seek help preparing for marriage or a life partnership from a helping professional (psychologist, clergy member, other), the relationship is routinely talked through as having two dimensions...

- managing, navigating, and enjoying the *present*, and

- looking to, envisioning, and building the *future*...

...with effective communication woven through it all.

However, anything with only two legs can get wobbly. Physically, we instinctively lean on something when standing for too long (a wall, a doorway). In old age, people often rely on a cane. So, too, a committed relationship can get "wobbly" if its only dimensions are the two noted above—present and future—even with effective communication.

When you think about it, why would people entering a life partnership commit to maintaining a two-dimensional relationship? Why would those who help people prepare for their life commitment provide coaching around a two-dimensional partnership when we are each a three-dimensional individual who:

- lives in the *present*,

- looks to the *future*, and

- brings along *everything* we ever experienced in our *past*—especially from our childhood—that we didn't know how to process back then?

It's not just what happens in a three-dimensional experience at a movie theater. As noted in the essay "The Kaleidoscope of Three-Dimensional Living," three-dimensional living is what real living is. It's what it means to be human. It's what it means to be alive.

Notes

Almost universally when life partners are experiencing discord, unsettledness in their shared life, their focus and the focus of the helping professionals to whom they might turn is on whatever's not being navigated appropriately today: how they're not being present to each other, how they're not communicating effectively, how they're not responding effectively to each other's needs, how they've lost shared dreams that unite and propel them forward, how they should relearn how to be with each other.

Even though the partners may repair some of what's gotten off track, and even though they may learn that they're simply not right for each other, the perspective that is seldom given any attention is that the discord and unsettledness are routinely—although unconsciously—acted-out stories from one partner's...

- early life emotional freezer, and

- weeds that had been planted in them by a parent and family members...

...often simultaneously from each one's subconscious freezer or collection of weeds.

If this perspective is not introduced, the decision for partners to remain together—or not—is missing something: the opportunity to discover that the noise in their relationship is likely the emotional noise once frozen by a child or planted within the child by a parent and family members, noise which finally feels able to unload itself in the safe harbor of the relationship.

> *The noise in their relationship is likely the emotional noise once frozen by a child or planted within the child by a parent and family members, noise which finally feels able to unload itself in the safe harbor of the relationship.*

How this unloading takes place is often hurtful, offensive, and unfair to the receiving partner. The receiving partner's purpose in the relationship is not to be the dumping ground, punching bag, or garbage can for these now defrosted or cropped-up hurts, offenses, and unfair experiences of the child the other person once was.

While it's optimal for the partner whose story is defrosting to own what's flash thawed from within them, decode it, understand it, explain it to the receiving partner, it can be a caring contribution of the receiving partner to catch the fact that thawing-out or

---

Notes

weed-cropping-up is indeed what's going on with their partner, to decode/decipher the acted-out behavior, and to do their best to understand the story that's being presented.

What has just been described can end up feeling like a one-way street of empathy. However, I have found that, although there are one-way street experiences like this, there's a significant reason why the receiving partner can resist doing such private understanding, why they can find the presenting childhood story of their partner so annoying to navigate.

Feelings being defrosted or weeds of false belief about self, the world, or life cropping up from within their partner are feelings and weeds from childhood that the receiving partner has stored within themself, too. Even if the early life *circumstances* were different, the heat/difficulty of one partner's story is often flash thawing or pulling up the weeds of similar feelings from the receiving partner's own childhood.

It's important to remember that the story being revealed is being *unconsciously* acted out to get it out. The person acting out is too afraid to consciously know what's happening. In this case, the receiving partner can choose to do the work solo to realize what's being communicated through the acting out. When the receiving partner does so, two things can happen:

1. The resulting demeanor in the receiving partner lets the acting-out partner whose story is unfolding feel heard and understood—unconsciously so—without any conversation about it ever taking place. It's a level of private understanding that impacts the receiving partner's facial expression, tone of voice, and even choice of words.

2. The receiving partner can live with what they've caught, decoded, and understood whether from their acting-out partner's childhood emotional freezer or from their partner's collection of childhood weeds. When the time feels right, they can share with their acting-out partner what they've come to understand about this most recent installment of their partner's childhood story—and very likely of their own childhood story, too.

The eventual conversation about what's been acted out is a wonderful place for you as partners to be. By a willingness to learn how to navigate this third dimension of being human—the realizing, decoding, and understanding of something from your or your partner's early life—you can feel the relief that can come from conversational sharing,

Notes

and you can treasure the resulting enhancement of an emotionally intimate connection between you.

You will experience the privilege of receiving the story of something that happened to your partner, how it made your partner feel, something so painful, unfair, baffling, and terrifying for the child your partner once was and had to navigate, that it could only be survived by keeping it hidden from themselves. These emotionally heavy, frozen stories have been carried by your partner for years, if not decades. The weeds from your partner's childhood have often choked the free flow of their life.

Again, a unique strengthening of intimacy can happen between you when one partner can experience the relief of sharing and the other the privilege of receiving.

> *A unique strengthening of intimacy can happen between you when one partner can experience the relief of sharing and the other the privilege of receiving.*

As has been noted, some people should simply not be together as life partners. Circumstances at the time the individuals met may have clouded their perspectives. And there are times when someone is unconsciously attracted to a person precisely because they'll receive a difficult experience to navigate similar to what they already had to navigate in their life with a parent or family member.

Example. Someone is drawn to a person with a substance use disorder. Unconsciously the MTT—Maybe This Time—virus may have been operative. Even if it looks like the similarity is to a previous romantic relationship, MTT related to one's parent or family members was most likely at play in the previous romantic relationship, too.

Maybe this time I can crack the code on navigating someone like my substance dependent parent. Maybe this time I can make a significant contribution to the life of someone like this. Maybe this time I can figure out how to have a relationship with someone who has these traits and make it work.

All these MTTs have been fueled by the false hope that—if I can triumph in some way this time—the pain I still carry from my parent or family member can be replaced

Notes

by a victory now. But that's not true. The baffling pain experienced from a parent or family member has a lifetime impact on us which we will forever be cleaning up when it defrosts or pulling as a weed when it crops up.

We've heard the observation, "Well, they were just attracted to something familiar in this person." Except for the second "i" in the word familiar, the first six letters in the word familiar spell the word *famili(y)*, and thus the unconscious pull to win now.

However, more often it's been my experience that an individual's radar, when being attracted to someone, goes beyond the unconscious wish to win now, beyond physical appeal, beyond enjoyment shared through experiences of meals, music, and other activities. It goes beyond how dreaming about and envisioning the future with this potential partner begins to take shape in one's mind and heart.

Our emotional radar also unconsciously picks up that this other person will understand what we'll be unpacking from our early life emotional freezer, will understand the cropped-up weeds we'll be sorting through, because this potential life partner has similar feelings within them.

Examples of this include the likelihood that each person was humiliated as a child, or perhaps each was given the impression that they meant little or nothing to a parent (even though many wonderful material things may have been routinely provided), or perhaps they were each made to feel less than within the family where they were growing up.

If you are to have the strongest foundation possible—like the tripod for a camera for good photography—it only makes sense for each of you to commit to and share a three-dimensional life with each other by:

Managing, navigating, and enjoying the **PRESENT**,

Looking to, envisioning, and building the **FUTURE**,

Recognizing, decoding, and understanding
the baffling, hurtful stories from each other's **PAST**,
from each person's childhood emotional freezer as they defrost,
or as they crop up like weeds in the relationship,
that is, each time a new truth surfaces and reveals
what it was like for each of you to be a child.

Notes

So many life partnerships don't continue because neither the partners nor the helping professionals have realized that struggles in a committed relationship are from the same source as struggles in an individual's life: from painful stories now coming out from the childhood emotional freezer or from among the childhood weeds of false belief about self, the world, or life of one or each partner. They come out often as a Number 3 experience, with partners often talking about their troubles as a "s##t storm." These words are truly precise when considering the concept of going Number 3.

It's always the unasked for, not invited, intrusive arrival of anything painful from childhood that makes already terribly difficult and heartbreaking times in the present even rougher and heavier for an individual and for life partners. As we add the unpacking of childhood to what's shared within a committed relationship, we will come to feel lighter over time and less and less burdened or stuck. Bit by bit, we will be moving out from within us truly heavy boxes of baffling, hurtful feelings, emptying and unpacking our childhood emotional freezer, sorting through childhood weeds that will forever crop up, lightening the load over time of what we've been carrying—silently and alone—for so very long.

Perhaps this is why the phrase *thinking outside the box* has become so commonly used. Maybe this has been an unconscious yet shared awareness that we haven't only been carrying heavy boxes or a packed childhood emotional freezer within, we've often been in the box or freezer, closer than we ever realized to those earliest life stories, close to the players in those stories. That's why staying in the box—why not thinking or living outside of the box—can unconsciously be appealing in a very personal way. Being in that box keeps us connected with and close to both the stories and to the people in those stories—even though they were hurtful to us.

So, how do partners learn to navigate the reality that their life partnership is as three-dimensional as every individual life? The same principle applies: *Struggle* always indicates that defrosting from the childhood emotional freezer of one or each member of the relationship is taking place—or that weeds from the childhood of one or each partner are cropping up, choking things out, overwhelming the garden of the relationship.

Defrosted childhood feelings or cropped-up childhood weeds might be something an individual experiences within, is conscious of, and then may talk out, and discuss with their partner. However, what happens most is that one partner unconsciously starts *acting out* to get out of themselves whatever has unconsciously defrosted or cropped up.

Notes

Whenever one person says to themselves, "Why am I acting like this? Why did I act like that?"—or if someone thinks or says this about their partner—whether it's about something said or done, not said, not done, an attitude, a silence, then this is proof that something has defrosted from a person's childhood freezer or cropped up from among that person's childhood weeds.

> *Whenever one person says to themselves,*
> *"Why am I acting like this? Why did I act like that?"*
> *—or if someone thinks or says this about their partner—*
> *this is proof that something has defrosted from a person's childhood freezer*
> *or cropped up from the person's childhood weeds.*

It takes ongoing practice and commitment to notice this in yourself, and it takes conscious openness to receive the observation from your partner that "you're acting out." Yes, something is going on today that triggers the defrosting, the cropping up, and the acting out that follows. However, even though a current catalyst has defrosted something from the childhood freezer or caused a weed from childhood to crop up, whatever has just defrosted or cropped up must be looked at first—chronologically first—or no real resolution of any issue today can take place.

Here are three examples of this:

Example 1. Someone is treating their partner as if they're worth nothing and is shocked to be told they are doing so. It turns out that, when the offending person was a child, they were often made to eat their food on the floor next to the dining room table. Really. It's not at all right that the offending person is making their partner feel like they're worth nothing, but now we have an insight into why this might unconsciously be happening.

The offending partner can never forget what their behavior is and from where it has come. And the hurt partner now knows, although at great expense to themself, a beyond words violation of dignity that was suffered by their life partner—unbelievably—at the hands of their partner's parent.

Example 2. Two life partners are each good people and very caring for their children. However, there seems to be a detachment between the partners, something that has gotten worse

---

Notes

over time. They're not mean to each other, just detached regarding time spent together and regarding their sexual intimacy, too.

One of the partners had parents who were more involved with each other than they were with their children. The other partner had a parent who had long workdays, did nothing with their children after work, and on days off socialized extensively with friends. Although circumstantially different, these two life partners have the exact same frozen files from childhood: files of detachment and MIA-ness by their parents.

In the safe harbor of this relationship, these sad and painful stories have been defrosting, have been acted out, but who knew? A new intimacy can be found for these life partners as their acted-out stories are identified for what they are and trustingly explained and shared—every time any detachment between them reappears.

Example 3. For clarity within this next example of life partners, one will be referred to as the caregiving partner, the other as the spouse.

A truly kind caregiving partner has been doing countless things for their aging parents even though the parents have never demonstrated any personal investment of care or interest in their generously caring child. The parents never tried to genuinely know their child either during the person's childhood nor as the adult they have become, basically treating their child like they didn't exist. One of the elderly parents once said they had been expecting their children to die before the parents did, perhaps a subtle confession of the parent wanting their children to be out of the way.

The spouse has witnessed the frequency with which their caregiving partner has been taken for granted by the aging parents: dismissed, devalued, never genuinely appreciated for the person they are—not as a child, not as the adult they are now.

However, the caregiving partner often felt like their spouse didn't truly have their back, wasn't actively supportive and caring when new demands for elder care would present themselves again and again. The caregiving partner felt treated by their spouse like they didn't exist, the same feelings their aging parents had always made them feel.

How could the spouse be so detached from all that their caregiving partner was going through with their aging parents? Here's what was being acted out:

Notes

The seemingly checked-out spouse was—as a child—also taken for granted, dismissed, devalued, never genuinely appreciated for the person they were. They were, in fact, treated like they didn't exist. So, to protect themself from the pain of this disregard and poor treatment from their parents, as a child the spouse would unconsciously cease to exist. By unconsciously being the one treating themself like they didn't exist, by unknowingly devaluing themself, and through a metaphorical hiding from their parents, the spouse created ways to protect themself from the awful pain caused by their parents.

So, when the caregiving partner was being made to feel by their spouse like they didn't exist, it wasn't being done to be mean or uncaring. The seemingly checked-out spouse was unconsciously—and with great care—protecting their caregiving partner by treating them like they didn't exist because this was the very strategy by which the spouse once protected themself from the terrible devaluing pain they experienced from their own parents during childhood.

This third dimension—navigating any pain from childhood as it intrudes into our life today—is the dimension of life most of us never knew has been simmering within, still alive, from forever. Consciously or unconsciously, we have thought and hoped our earliest past was all neatly packed away, safely stored forever. That's why so few life partners ever incorporate this third dimension of being human into their shared life.

However, including this dimension of living into a shared life enhances a life partnership to make it the strongest, the most rewarding, and the most peace-giving. Over time, partners will find they are living the emotionally richest of all relationships: a three-dimensional one.

So, these are my wishes for you...

First Wish. That you live as a team to support each other when—as indicated by struggle—your emotional systems are reminding you that you are three-dimensional persons, when emotional "noise" stored long ago in your childhood emotional freezers is defrosting and presenting itself in its raw pain today. It was pain that was too much for you to deal with as children, the very reason you had to flash freeze it during childhood. Or the noise may be early life weeds once again cropping up.

Second Wish. That you recognize times of struggle as most likely the simultaneous surfacing of childhood pain from within each of you—your pain and your partner's—whether

---

Notes

they're painful feelings that you each unconsciously flash froze as a child, or whether they're the weeds of false belief about yourself, the world, or life planted within you in childhood by a parent or family members and cropping up now.

Third Wish. That you listen together to these defrosting feelings and the cropped-up weeds from childhood. This will enhance your shared intimacy and is the only thing that will return you to effective footing for navigating whatever the issue at hand really is, whether it's about something today or something related to planning for the future.

Fourth Wish. That you not weaponize this understanding of our emotional dynamics by being snide when your partner is acting out something from their childhood that's defrosted or a weed from your partner's childhood that has cropped up. Is it easy to be on the receiving end of your partner's acted-out story? By no means. But if it's not easy for you to experience this childhood pain from your partner when it's landing on you, what was it like for your partner to experience and navigate this pain when they were only a child? This is not to give your partner an excuse for their acting out, but as a team, these are experiences to unpack and process together.

Once we understand that each of us as an individual is a three-dimensional person— managing the present, building the future, unpacking our childhood past—each of us can navigate the constant, kaleidoscopic shifting from one dimension to another which every moment is. Why wouldn't we want to live our individual life in this three-dimensional richness? It would be living in the moment in the fullest sense.

And once we understand that a life partnership is also three-dimensional, why as partners wouldn't we want to integrate the life navigation skills associated with this dynamic into our shared life? Our committed relationship would become the richest possible and continue ever more so over time.

> *Once we understand that a life partnership is also three-dimensional,*
> *why as partners wouldn't we want to integrate*
> *the life navigation skills associated with this dynamic into our shared life?*
> *Our committed relationship would become the richest possible*
> *and continue ever more so over time.*

Notes

These may be new concepts, I know. But if you are brave enough to trust them, the return on your investment of emotional bravery and care will be a beautiful one.

Take care.

Ted

Notes

12. To Parents

(Teachers: This letter will apply to you in many ways, too.)

To Parents:

The responsibilities you have regarding your children can seem daunting. You are responsible for your children's physical safety, health care, nutrition, shelter, education, clothing, and more. You are "on" to provide these to each child 24/7 for a minimum of eighteen years—eighteen years!—and in so many families, far beyond eighteen years. The time, energy, and financial resources this demands from you are untold. You just keep on providing, because the needs are always there, and often the needs of more than one child are calling for your awareness.

Not that you ever want to be negligent in any of these areas of care for your child or children, but children are remarkably able to put things into perspective when—for legitimate reasons—one or more of the dimensions of physical and logistical care as noted above can't be provided or can't be there as the child or parent would most like them to be.

Children learn early-on that things and services cost money—for example, clothes, school supplies, food, housing—and they therefore understand to varying degrees why some things can't be provided to them or for the family. However, children can also sense negligence in these areas, and when they do, it's a bafflement that is traumatic for them.

With that said, what children cannot put into perspective is when the core responsibility of a parent—that wouldn't cost a penny—is not provided: assuring that each child feels good about themself because they feel safe in the world, peaceful and confident being who they are, and as a result, treasured. When a child feels treasured, they can feel at home with themself.

Every child knows—as early as when they're a toddler—that anything not treasured or valued in the house is not safe and could be thrown away. So, unless a child feels valued and of interest to a parent as the person the child is by what they experience in their regard from a parent's behaviors, words, looks, attitudes, tones of voice, and even silences, the child can't feel safe, comfortable, or good being themself.

Notes

> *Unless a child feels valued and of interest to their parents as the person they are, the child can't feel safe.*

Each time—consciously or not—a child experiences not feeling safe or valued, it's a moment of fear, bafflement, and hurt. It threatens their very existence.

These are the moments that a child—of any age—flash freezes and stores in their mind, heart, and body because they have nowhere else to put these feelings, no place else to keep any weeds of false belief that have been planted in them by a parent or family members. A child may act out some of them, but most of them are kept in storage after unconsciously being flash frozen and kept in hiding—every child's instinctive way to suspend the painful moment in time and move forward with their day, with their life.

Whenever you say about your child, "They're really acting out today!"—or when you ask them the question, "Why are you acting like that?"—you are experiencing your child's emotional system unconsciously engaging the third form of communication: acting something *out*. We have all come to rely on words alone to a counterproductive degree. We unconsciously limit our concept of communication to what someone writes out in whatever form and to what someone talks out with us in a conversation.

So, what is your child acting out? As was explained in the essay "Literal Language Telling the Truth," one of the unconscious purposes of someone acting out is to not only *tell* a story but also to get the receiver of the communication to *feel* the story. What your child leaves you feeling by what they are acting out—confused, frustrated, disoriented, hurt, afraid, disrespected, "what will happen next," exhausted, helpless, hopeless—is the story your child is telling you because they either don't have the skills or don't have the confidence to share with you in any other way.

It may be about something they are currently experiencing. It might be about something they had experienced once or multiple times earlier in their life, an experience they didn't know what to do with, something they flash froze within themself, something which is coming into the light of day now. It might be the weed of a false belief or presumption that you or another family member unknowingly planted in your child. It might be something about you that they don't know how to tell you. It's left to you

Notes

to connect the dots, bravely knowing that the story being acted out may be about an impact on your child by you or another family member. Here are three examples:

Example 1. You are unsure why your very good child is so filled with self-doubt. You are doubting your own ability to help your child. You are feeling lost because your child never believes they're truly doing something right, never believes they're genuinely a good person. Yes, you're feeling unsure and lost.

It may be hard for your child to call to mind—and hard for you to call to mind, too—that perhaps you are the one—right along with much good that you've done for your child— who once or often have made them feel unsure and lost, full of self-doubt.

There was a time when you made them feel ashamed because a schoolmate was showing some romantic interest in them. Or there was the time when your child tried helping you with a task, but you made them feel stupid by things you said when they didn't do something like you thought they would.

Unsure, lost, full of self-doubt.

Example 2. You are baffled as to how to energize a child who seems to have little motivation to manage and live their own life. However, when you look at what this child (of whatever age, be it seven or thirty) is doing, your child may be mirroring the lack of motivation in life that they see in you.

You have abdicated living your life by only going to work and then sitting on the couch watching TV when you're not working. You're investing nothing in your marriage. Your child has been baffled about how to help energize you.

So, keeping you company in your lack of personal care and simultaneously mirroring for you how you look: these are two ways your child has unconsciously found to be of service to you, someone about whom they so genuinely care. Your child both keeps you company and mirrors how you look as you abdicate living your life—especially because none of your other children seem to care much personally about you at all.

Example 3. In the "Letter to Life Partners," there was the story of the parents who loved their children but were also acting out the emotionally detached families in which they each grew up. One of their children started exhibiting a detaching from self by turning to

---

Notes

drugs. This child was mirroring for their parents what detachment from self and others looks like.

Examples such as these are not times to rush into having a conversation with your child, not times to share the insights you have about how your child is acting. Your child is acting out because they don't know the words for talking it out, might be afraid to even hear the words, and simply may not want to talk about it.

Engage private understanding to decipher what your child is acting out. Listen within yourself first. Live with what you have deciphered, as uncomfortable as it may be to do so. If you are not a single parent, discuss it with your partner, be this your child's biological parent or not. Doing so will help you catch your breath and have better footing for whatever direction, discipline, or coaching is appropriate and necessary for you to provide to your child.

Remember the ways to decipher what someone is acting out:

1. Listen to the words you use to describe your child's behavior: confused, lost, secretive, inappropriate, resistant, or controlling. They can lead you to connect the dots regarding which experience of their life—current, earlier life, or both—that your child is getting *out* by dramatizing it.

2. Identify what your child is making you feel—lost, hurt, frustrated, helpless, rejected—to name a few. Then ask yourself—not your child—what your child might be telling you: something they are feeling about the break-up of a friendship they are going through, about getting bullied at school, perhaps about feeling not understood by you at some point in the past, perhaps their helplessness about something they see you doing.

Writing out these clues on paper will help you to better fit the puzzle pieces together.

This is hard to do while the acting out is taking place, but even if you do the deciphering later, it will bring you better footing. With better footing, your own instinctive creativity for how best to parent your child in this situation will flow and surface all on its own—more than you might have ever imagined.

Again, it may seem odd to not share your insights with your child within a conversation. But there are times when conversation is not appropriate, when just listening within, private understanding, private knowing, is what's most caring and appropriate.

Notes

There are times when we may have visited a funeral home or memorial service to comfort a friend grieving the loss of someone in their life. Sometimes we say nothing and just give them a hug. Such private understanding is very caring, even powerful, and what's just right for the situation. The same is true when listening to what your children may be communicating with you through acting out.

Discipline, coaching, or teaching may, of course, be needed because we're talking about your eighteen-year-old or younger child (coaching that's important for an older child, too), but first use private understanding to quietly hold your child—and what they may be suffering—in your heart. The right words and actions will surface from within you in the right way, at the right time. You can't even plan these words. Very often this will happen without having a specific conversation in words about what you came to understand about your child while doing your private understanding.

> *Use private understanding to quietly hold your child*
> *—and what they may be suffering—in your heart.*

Example. *Parents were very concerned about their child—whom they dearly loved—who was a junior in high school. The child seemed negligent regarding schoolwork and regarding any consistent communication with the parents. They tried many different ways to coach their child about the importance of academics and about how much they wanted some proactive communication from their child. The parents were feeling angry, hurt, and rejected.*

Once the parents looked at both their child's behavior and the feelings the child's behavior was triggering in them, they realized that their child was struggling with a romantic interest. The person the child was dating was struggling with their self-esteem, neglecting school, and using drugs as a result. Their child was trying so hard to provide support, interest, patience, and generous coaching to this friend. However, none of their child's best efforts were making any difference, perhaps like a time the child once tried to get through to their parents, couldn't, and felt angry, hurt, and rejected.

Over a few days, their child unconsciously sensed a different level of understanding on the part of the parents. The "vibe" in the house was different. The parents' tone of voice had adjusted itself without any conscious effort on their part to do so. Private understanding caused helpful, unconscious shifts within each parent, and it freed them to think consciously in some new ways, too.

Notes

After those few days, the child participated willingly and productively for almost two hours in a substantive and non-defensive conversation with their parents.

One of the reasons that decoding your child's acting out may be difficult to do—just as it may be difficult to do with a life partner—is that the story your child is telling, the pain they are asking you to feel with them, may be a pain that you yourself once had to feel as a child. Perhaps you tried to positively influence a friend, sibling, or parent who was going through a rough time, but everything you tried was dismissed. You felt angry, hurt, and rejected. The heat of your child's situation today has defrosted your own, old, similar pain.

> **The story your child is telling,**
> **the pain they are asking you to feel with them,**
> **may be a pain that you yourself once had to feel as a child.**

It's important to remember this if you're *struggling* to hear your child's story. You will personally be the richer for it, and your child will have someone who genuinely knows what they are going through.

People of all ages unconsciously play the "game"—and children especially so—"I won't listen to you until I sense that you have listened to me." It's important for your child's development and safety, of course, that they listen to you. You have every right to expect them to take your coaching seriously.

However, navigating the dynamic of listening to what a child is communicating to you by what they are acting out will give you better footing for what is yours to teach. They will sense that you have been listening to them. It will give your child the security that their parent isn't afraid to hear and know what's being shared—even if it's about a negative impact on your child once made by you or someone else within or outside of the family.

Someone once asked me, "Aren't there simply some rotten kids?" I don't think there are. Kids are people. They are acting out stories about things they don't understand, don't know what to do with, regarding themself and their emotions, what they see in parents and family members, what they are navigating in the world beyond their home, what they may sense as an emotional virus within the wider family system, something that may be passed on from generation to generation.

Notes

So, no, I don't believe there are naturally rotten kids. Kids—like all people—act out the baffling and painful stories they don't know what to do with, stories that have been stored within them either as feelings they flash froze or as weeds that you or other family members unknowingly planted in them.

What we're focusing on here is in the category of *not costing a penny*, the most important and critical of what a parent provides for their child. When a child experiences personal, non-monetary investment in them on the part of a parent, it means the world to the child. Nothing is more important. Nothing helps a child feel safer in the world and more confident in and at home with themself.

Being grounded in your core responsibility of helping each child feel safe in the world, confident in and at home with themself, is no easy task. Doing this changes every year. It may be done a certain way when a child is one year old, but then it will be done differently when they're two, and then when they're three, and as they continue to grow. It changes in an ongoing way all the way through eighteen years old and beyond. Staying in synch with a child's growing self is why the skill of deciphering what someone is acting out is one that will get ongoing use.

We all act out to varying degrees across the course of our life. Children of whatever age act out. You as parents act out, too, because each of you was once a child. Each of you has frozen childhood experiences that will flash thaw and early life weeds that will crop up from time to time.

This dynamic is multiplied when there's a multi-generational family living under the same roof. Co-residents on every level of the generations will be contributing to the acting-out swirl of life in that house. Remembering how to decipher and interpret any communication that's being acted out is of value in all important relationships—including multi-generational relationships within a single household.

Private understanding—*listening* to what people act out—will serve us well in so many ways.

Take care.

Ted

Notes

13. To Young People

To Young People in College, High School, and Junior High:

The process of growing up can include a lot of fun and adventure. It includes the hard work of academics, and it also brings with it the challenges that are part of getting to know yourself, who you are, what you want for your life in the future. It includes what we enjoy about our relationships with a parent, family members, friends, classmates, and romantic interests. It also includes many things that keep our relationships with any of these people from being as smooth as we might like them to be.

Depending on how much of this collection of writing you have read prior to reading this letter, you will know to varying degrees what my understanding is of the struggling we experience in life. *Struggling* is always a fight inside us between the impact of something today defrosting something from our early life that we once unconsciously flash froze and stored within us. Or a current situation may cause old weeds of false belief about ourself, the world, or life once planted in us by a parent or family members to crop up today. Both the defrosted feelings and the cropped-up weeds are experiences from earlier times in our life with which we didn't know what to do. They've been unconsciously stored within us.

> *Struggling is always a fight inside us*
> *between something today defrosting something from our early life*
> *that we once unconsciously flash froze and stored within us*
> *or something today that's causing weeds of false belief*
> *unconsciously stored within us to crop up now.*

The defrosted feelings or cropped-up weeds are all from earlier times in our life. They are experiences of bafflement caused by a parent or other members of our family— whether these were caused by them consciously or not. It's the showing up today of hurt, fear, confusion, harshness, abandonment, the experience of someone being there but not really being there—and more—that were painful impacts on us when we were children, even babies, even in the womb.

Notes

Whether we flash froze feelings in childhood or whether a parent or family members early in our life planted weeds of false belief about ourself, the world, or life itself, we stored them all for one reason: we were children. We didn't know what to do with them or make of them. We didn't know how to do emotional calculus, didn't know how to arrive at psychological understandings and insights regarding our parent and family members. And we didn't want to think badly about our parent or families.

So, our unconscious storing of experiences and what they felt like was an instinctive and helpful thing to do at those times. It's just that no one ever explained to us that:

- Anything we once flash froze within—or any weeds that were once planted within us—will want to be freed, will want us to sort through them.

- The releasing process will happen across our lifetime and is at play whenever we are struggling with something.

For example, what might the story be when someone is struggling with their schoolwork? The story might be many things, but some possibilities for the unconscious story behind this struggle with academics might be:

Example 1. "I always craved some individual investment of time and energy from a parent. Their helping me with my homework could provide that."

Example 2. "I knew my parent placed great value on my schoolwork, but I always felt there were more important things in life such as 'not what I know in school, but how well you as my parent know me, how well we know each other in this family.' So, I can fairly easily blow off my schoolwork as not important because I'm trying to get my parent to understand and focus on something more important to me than schoolwork."

Example 3. "There was so much emotional bafflement going on in our house that my brain was saturated every day: perhaps parents fighting with each other, perhaps a war between a parent and a sibling, perhaps a sick relative living in the house. I arrived at school each day with a packed brain, and I came home with an even more packed brain. Because I was so worried—consciously and unconsciously—about the emotional and other types of turmoil in our house, schoolwork paled in comparison, and I didn't have any room to take in anything else."

Notes

It's not easy for any of us to come to understand the impacts—intentional or not—of a parent and family on us. It's not easy at all. However, if you are willing to do so, you can practice understanding this bit by bit over time.

> *It's not easy for any of us to come to understand*
> *the impacts of a parent and family on us.*
> *It's not easy at all.*

This is not something you will necessarily have to discuss with a parent. It is, however, something you can build up strength to know privately. You can ask a trustworthy person such as a counselor at school to serve as a support for you in what you have to know about a parent or family member and their conscious or unconscious impacts on you. Remember: one reason we've kept "stuff" to ourself is that many of us know that talking with a parent or family member—especially about negative things involving them as they related to us—usually hasn't gotten us very far.

My major concern about what you are struggling with is this: I don't want you to think of yourself as the problem or that there's something wrong with you. All of us have collected problems along the way in life and have unconsciously stored them within our childhood emotional freezer. Some exist as weeds of false belief about ourself or about life planted by a parent or family members. So, it's important for each of us to become skilled at sorting through both the frozen items and the weeds.

The actual problem is that no one ever informed us of the dynamics of our emotional life. No one ever taught us how to navigate it. Not knowing about our childhood emotional freezer nor about weeds planted in us by a parent or family members is something I wish would diminish and, optimally, be eliminated over time. However, for now, remember: you are not the problem or a problem.

Sometimes we think we are the problem—and sometimes we even become the problem—for reasons such as these:

- as a cover and diversion for what the problem really is—something wrong about how a parent and family members have regarded and treated us—and how we've had to live as a result;

- to invalidate our good and genuine self, unconsciously believing that doing

Notes

this will hurt less than feeling invalidated by a parent and family members regarding who and how we are;

- to comply with a message that we might have received about ourself that we are a burden to a parent, or that being pregnant with us was a surprise to a parent, and not a very convenient one; or

- as a way to be connected to a parent if we've found it baffling about how to do so in any other way because, if we share a perception of ourself that our parent has about us, we have something in common with them, have found a connection with that parent—as desperate a way as it may be to achieve this connection.

Because we were children, we absolutely needed connection with a parent and family members. Nothing is more important to a child. So, we unconsciously seek this connection however we can get it, even if by the desperate default of believing that I am a problem or *the* problem, or that I have a problem, even if this connection is unconsciously manufactured and a false one.

This sounds, I know, like quite a dissing of parents and family members. And these explanations of where our inappropriate behaviors and the emotions we struggle with come from can sound like excuses for what we're not managing well in our lives.

The point of all this, however, is to help us bravely acknowledge how a parent and family members have impacted us. The struggles of our life are evidence of these baffling and even painful impacts. As we come to know what we're navigating, we'll be able to mop up what defrosts from within us, unpack what's being uncovered, weed out what's overwhelming and tripping us up, and free our natural agency to both responsibly carry ourself through the day and carry ourself effectively through life.

I also don't want you to be in search of a word that categorizes you with a problem or a *condition*, words such as depressed, anxious, having ADHD, and others. Wanting to have a "condition" is a common trend among young people. Sometimes this is to make someone feel less alone and feel belonging and connection with others. Sometimes it's to get special accommodations for classes or testing.

Whatever the reason, I don't want you making a label or category part of your identity. Doing so is cuddling with something not helpful for you and diverts you from bravely

---

Notes

understanding and from owning what you really have to know about your emotional struggling—something that you truly owe to yourself.

It's also so important to understand what's going on inside of you and why, where your struggles are coming from, and how to manage them because—unless we bravely own the baffling and painful impacts of parent and family members on us (in addition to any impacts by them for which we are grateful)—we can *unconsciously* look for a dating partner similar to our parent or family member to fill the holes or sooth the inside wounds left by them—but no one can do that.

Remember: it's all unconscious, but we want to make the baffling and hurtful impact on us by a parent or family member go away by winning or *cracking the code* in a relationship with someone somehow like them. If we can figure it out with a new inner circle person, we unconsciously think we won't have to process the baffling impacts and hurts we experienced from any original inner circle person or persons.

"If I can navigate, survive, or make it work with someone like the parent (or other family member) who so baffled me, then maybe the pain that's been stored in me will all go away." But that's just not how it works with the flash-frozen emotions from our early life nor with the weeds of false belief about ourself, about the world, about life that were planted in us by a parent or family member. We can get attracted to someone like a parent or family member partly because they're familiar to us, but mostly because we can be taken over by the MTT (Maybe This Time) emotional virus.

So, we have to be aware every day of what might be defrosting from within us and of each time an early life weed may crop up today. If we integrate these skills into how we live, our choice of a dating, romantic, and possible life partner will be about what's right us and right for them, not unconsciously about how to fix what wasn't right with a parent or family member or about trying to get from someone else what we didn't get from our parent or family member.

There's an additional benefit for people of any age who do this work. By deciphering struggles as the unmasking of the negative impacts of a parent and our family members on us, we then logically ask about them:

- Why are they acting like this?
- What are they acting out?

Notes

- What is their story?

We come to understand the story of the people at the root of our struggles. We come to understand them like never before...

- where they came from in life,

- what they lived through, and

- how their early life impacted them...

...whether or not we get to have a conversation with them about their own life story. What may look like dissing or blaming is simply following the breadcrumbs of our own story, and it will help us follow the breadcrumbs of the stories of a parent and other family members, too.

You may not want to begin processing what you struggle with and what baffles you in life in this way, but when you do, it will serve you well.

Take care.

Ted

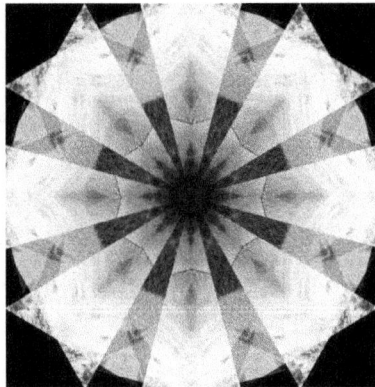

Notes

14. To Resistors

To Anyone Who Resists Doing Their Personal Work:

There is nothing easy for any of us about doing our personal work to better understand and know ourself. Whenever we're *struggling* with anything—our self-worth or self-confidence, a relationship, a work issue, even health issues—something's being thawed out from our childhood emotional freezer, or a weed of false belief about ourself, the world, or life planted in childhood is cropping up now. Each collides with, intrudes upon, piggybacks on something currently going on in our life. Fine-tuning our emotional reflexes to catch when this is happening—and strengthening our emotional muscles to hold what we've caught—will diffuse the struggling.

However, sometimes a person doesn't want to diffuse their struggling. Sometimes a person doesn't want to decipher, decode, unpack their struggling and, by doing so, quiet it. At first, this doesn't make sense, and yet there is a logic to this choice, be it a conscious one or not.

The logical presumption is that the diffusing of a struggle—to whatever degree—will be the loss of that struggle. What an unconsciously odd concept for some people: the loss of that struggle. So, why might someone not want to be ever more free from the struggle created by defrosted truths or cropped-up weeds from childhood that have attached themselves to something today? Why might someone not want to be freer each day from this heavy dynamic which keeps them in turmoil?

The feelings we had to flash freeze as a child to get through them were the baffling, hurtful experiences we had with either a parent or other members of our family. Or these baffling hurts were weeds planted by a parent and family members. Whichever they were, they weren't good experiences and feelings, and they didn't make sense to us. We didn't know what to do with certain feelings except flash freeze them and store them in our childhood emotional freezer. If they were weeds of false belief about ourself and about life, we buried them in our subconscious. These experiences—consciously or not—had a significant impact on us.

Every child wants to say that their parent and/or family had a big, significant impact on them. So, even if the big and significant impact was baffling hurt, fear, or an experience

---

Notes

of being devalued, we may unconsciously want to keep the grip this impact has on us because it's the biggest thing we ever received from a parent or from another member of our family. Unconsciously, we may want to hold onto it even if it's emotional turmoil of one kind or another and to whatever degree.

When not being able to break through with these concepts when working with a client, I've asked myself, "Are they lazy?" or "Are they afraid?" The answer to each question is anchored in the same truth: one's parent and family. If a parent and family members were lazy in their regard and treatment of us, then a way to be connected to them is to be lazy in our regard and treatment of ourself. If our struggle—finding a sense of self, our search for peace, whatever it might be—is the most impactful thing we ever received from them, then we may indeed be resistant and even afraid to no longer have that struggle because it was *from them* and continues to connect us *to them*.

> *If our struggle—finding a sense of self, our search for peace, whatever it might be—is the most impactful thing that we ever received from a parent or family member, then we may indeed be resistant and even afraid to no longer have that struggle because it was from them and continues to connect us to them.*

Consider these two examples:

Example 1. *A person is terribly burdened by situations in their work life, they seldom if ever take time off, and they often have no energy left to relax with their partner on the weekend. In fact, on the weekend they work themself to the bone doing projects around the house.*

When it's suggested that they be gentler with themself, the words are appreciated but really of little interest to the person. When it's suggested that they are being loyal to what their parents gave them to feel about themself—that they deserve nothing better than to be a prisoner to responsibilities in life in one form or another—they don't want to consider it. When it's suggested that they do some writing when they feel the most churned inside in order to get "stuff" out, they get annoyed at the suggestion.

Notes

This person had a parent with whom they could never find their footing and feel genuinely close. Their parent was routinely more engaged with being a martyr than with being connected to their children. The parent worked hard professionally, seemed to feel terribly burdened by their children, and in their mind was without sufficient support from their spouse. In truth, this parent was not only actively engaged with being a martyr but loved being one.

Is it any wonder that the child became someone who also gravitated to being a martyr both at work and at home? It was this person's desperate way to have a connection with, have something in common with, be on the same team as their martyr parent. Nothing and no one were going to take away from them what they had finally found as their connection—although a desperate, hostage-taking connection—to their elusive parent.

<u>Example 2</u>. Someone is a descendent within a family system where their ancestors suffered greatly through physical torture and political oppression. This person's compassion is so generous that they've unconsciously carried the sufferings of their ancestors within them in a genuinely heartfelt way, and it expresses itself through rage at political impacts on societies.

They also had a parent who was irresponsible to them in many ways throughout childhood. The parent subjected their child to repeated humiliation through their own belittling regard and treatment of their child and through truly rough medical and psychological interventions. The impacts from the parent's belittling treatment and from the medical and psychological interventions have been dealt with for years through what seems like an endless search for answers. This person has suffered greatly—physically and emotionally—but has never known what to do with their suffering and its aftermath impacts.

Unconsciously, this person has leveraged their childhood realities of physical suffering, emotional turmoil, and rage at political issues to give them connection and purpose: a desperate connection to their hurtful parent and simultaneously a noble purpose of solidarity with their physically tortured and politically oppressed ancestors.

Because this person has found connection and purpose through compounded physical suffering, ongoing emotional torture, and political rage, the prospect of feeling some relief, of being gentle with themself, and of living a slower and simpler life has become threatening for them. Living without such connection and purpose is both terrifying and of little actual interest to this person even though they may say otherwise.

Notes

If you are resistant to doing your personal work, I ask you to give some thought to the ideas I have shared with you in this collection of letters and essays, and especially within this particular letter. Perhaps reread "Essay 10: A Mission of Loyalty." If you begin unpacking your struggles, identifying defrosted feelings you had once flash frozen in childhood, it will indeed be a life-long process. If you learn how to weed what's choking you out in life, it's something you will be doing across your lifetime whenever any of the weeds from your childhood crop up.

You will never be without your memories of parent and family members, who they were, who they weren't, and never without more of these memories surfacing over time. These will be your forever connection to a parent, family members, and maybe also to your ancestral family system.

Some of your memories may be truly positive, but the ones that have the biggest impact on us are the baffling, painful ones. They will present themselves throughout life in the forms of defrosting, flooding feelings and choking, overwhelming weeds.

However, remaining a hostage to the baffling life experiences that a parent, family members, or your ancestral family system gave you does not have to be the way you are held by them or the way you hold onto them. You can hold them all in your memory and be less held by what baffled you about any of them.

You can then instead hold yourself and your life in a new way and feel a bit freer each day, but it's your resistance that's keeping you from this new experience of life.

> *You can hold yourself and your life in a new way*
> *and feel a bit freer each day,*
> *but it's your resistance*
> *that's keeping you from this new experience of life.*

I wish for you greater freedom each day from any devaluing ways you unconsciously let a parent or your family members—whether they are alive or dead—continue to hold you. I wish for you greater freedom from any desperate ways you unconsciously continue to hold them. I wish for you greater freedom from the biggest things they gave you if those biggest things are devaluing to you.

Notes

Again, you will forever hold a parent and family members in memory, but you no longer have to hold or be held by a parent, family members, or ancestral family system either through solidarity with how they suffered or by the ways they disregarded and poorly treated you.

> *You no longer <u>have to</u> hold or be held by a parent,*
> *family members, or ancestral family system*
> *either through solidarity with how they suffered*
> *or by the ways they disregarded and poorly treated you.*

Take care.

Ted

Notes

15. To Helping Professionals

To Helping Professionals—Medical Professionals, Mental Health Professionals, Social Workers, and Members of Other Helping Professional Communities:

The work that you and I do is such personal work with each and every patient or client. Our work is energy-draining—mentally, emotionally, and physically—for us and for those to whom we provide service. We have studied extensively and have done our best to keep our knowledge up to date.

However, I am concerned about the model in which so many of us work. It's a model of pathology, illness. The Diagnostic and Statistical Manual of Mental Disorders (the DSM) is an anchor for this model, a resource that offers valuable perspective on the emotional and behavioral patterns demonstrated by our patients and clients.

However, I don't believe there are enough helping professionals who invest the time and energy to understand a patient's/client's emotional experiences and behavioral patterns. The person is routinely understood from the perspective of the DSM, and I'm not sure how well they're understood from the perspective of themselves.

As I have noted in this collection of letters and essays, every feeling someone has is real, and every example of acting out is an alternate form of communication, someone telling a story, their life story. Strong emotions do not equal illness, and not every feeling that's flooding someone today is about today. In fact, acted-out stories are not about today, and every time someone is struggling, they are experiencing the rawness of an early life experience. It has found its way into the light of today after being in dark storage for a long time.

> *Every time someone is struggling,*
> *they are experiencing the rawness of an early life experience.*
> *It has found its way into the light of today*
> *after being in dark storage for a long time.*

There is good intention in wanting someone to experience a significant degree of relief from anxiety, panic, sadness, lack of self-worth, and other terrible feelings which

---

Notes

can flood and dominate a person. However, there is no real relief if, through freedom-promising medication and interventional techniques, the feelings get paused, put into a coma or napping state, or if they are leaped over, by-passed. Medication can often put feelings into a muffled state. Techniques that promise freedom from upset can bypass the emotions. However, if the feelings of one's painful, baffling, early life stories are not allowed to come out, they remain in the only place they have to stay: within the person.

Then, whether they are comatose, napping emotions or by-passed feelings, they will begin to emerge, try to come out again. All too often when this happens medication levels get increased to either quiet down or lift a mood. A medication may be substituted with a new one. And sometimes a new medication is introduced into a person's system in addition to other medications already there.

Because each person's chemistry is unique, everyone's body is like that cartoon image of a scientist with wild and crazy hair who is adding more and more substance to a smoke-billowing beaker. Each person's system can be reactive like the contents of that beaker.

People then navigate and sometimes suffer through the violent chemical activity going on within them. It may not always look violent, especially if someone becomes calmer due to a medication. However, a war within will begin at some point because the comatose, napping feelings will begin to wake up. The by-passed feelings will not want to remain—in fact, will resist—being sidelined. They'll want *out*.

So, why isn't every effort made to help these difficult feelings flow out rather than continuing to sequester them within? To what degree do you and I listen to a person's early life story as it presents itself in the raw and difficult emotions of today, feelings that pick up now from exactly where they were once paused, flash frozen? To what degree are we supporting our patients and clients in listening to their early life stories: the content, the defrosted and raw feelings, and the weeds that were planted in childhood and continue to crop up?

Being an enlightened witness to the intense emotional suffering of each person we are trying to serve is by no means easy. So, it's important to remember that, in the world of emotions, the adjective *intense* (when used to describe an emotion) equals the word *deep* equals the word *old*. By remembering this, we can support our patients and clients as they begin to understand what's been in storage within them nearly forever and making noise—assaulting them—today.

Notes

It takes courage for the helping professional to follow a more person-focused path of support for patients/clients. Some of us don't take this path because we genuinely want to provide the quickest possible relief through various medications and techniques. However, if we look for the quickest fix, we are not taking seriously what's surfacing in a person: the early life stories for which the time has come for unpacking and sorting.

Perhaps some of us don't follow a more person-focused path of service for our patients and clients because we are unconsciously motivated by a sense of power as a helper. Feeling some power now may be compensating for our own early life story, the story of being powerless in the face of the painful bafflements that were our own as children. Perhaps some of us don't take a more person-focused path because, if we did, we would have to *practice what we preach* and come to terms with our own early life stories.

My hunch is that most helping professionals have developed the passion for what they do because their own childhood story—be it conscious or not—has created an internal mission to alleviate emotional pain for others. The helping professional themself very likely knows all too well how awful such pain can be.

> *The helping professional themself*
> *very likely knows all too well*
> *how awful such pain can be.*

If we helping professionals truly owned our own personal, early life stories, we could provide improved support as our patients and clients move through the process of owning theirs. If we could come to understand that whatever is acted out by us or anyone else is the telling of a person's childhood story, our work would be so much less diagnostic, and less label-based. We would begin to think through things in less cluttered ways and use simpler language, for example:

Example 1. *Perhaps a person with social anxiety disorder is someone whose fear of social situations today is shouting the story that, as they began life in the house into which they were born, they lived on yellow alert—and maybe worse—each and every day because of the unpredictability of a parent, because of a parent's great sadness or flaring rage, because of a bullying sibling from whom a parent offered no protection.*

Notes

Example 2. Perhaps someone identified as bi-polar is reflecting the emotional whiplash they experienced routinely within their family when they were a child.

Example 3. Perhaps the child (or adult) with ADD or ADHD is acting out a story because they can't find the words to sit down and converse about it with someone. The child's parent may seem wonderful—and indeed may be so in many ways. They may be genuinely well-meaning. But there might be much emotional unsettledness going on within the home. It might be subtle or glaring. It might be the illness of a parent, sibling, or grandparent. Perhaps there are financial pressures or interpersonal discord within the house. The child's neighborhood might not feel safe. The child may simply be taking in a huge volume of disparate and unclear information day after day.

The child then arrives in the classroom with their mind already so full that they can't take in much additional information. They are so used to being on alert that being on alert is the primary task even in the classroom. Everything else is secondary. Because no one asks the parent about their impact or the impact of their household on their child, the child becomes the one with a problem.

Example 4. Much has been written about the toll on many students and adults from the isolation and lack of socialization during the COVID-19 Pandemic. There were challenges navigating this period in history for sure, and for many the loss of not being with schoolmates or workmates was a challenge.

However, perhaps when challenge became struggle for some, the impact of the pandemic was more because of where individuals were trapped for so long. Perhaps for some students, this was being 24/7 with the very people who made their day-to-day life so unsettled and unpeaceful with no respite from such difficult home situations by going to school. Perhaps for some adults, the emotional difficulty/heat of being at home was defrosting significant early life records within their childhood emotional freezers, thawing out frozen pain of what it was like for them to be at home as a child.

Example 5. Might this also be what's behind SAD (Seasonal Affective Disorder)? Perhaps SAD is the annual thawing out of frozen childhood memories when young people were trapped with the very persons and situations that made life so baffling and unsettling for them without the relief of being outside through longer days, without being able to spend time with diversionary people and activities.

Notes

Whether it's depression (weighed down), anxiety (churned up), or ADD (can't keep up with all that's going on), once again there's every reason to believe that each person's experience of being a child is what most impacts them later in life whether during a pandemic, with the onset of something like SAD as winter begins each year, and regarding so many other life experiences.

Moving to greater simplicity in our work—that is, knowing and understanding each person and their story—is a respect due every person whom we serve.

A broad spectrum of approaches—medication and others—are used to quiet the eruptions of these early life stories within patients and clients. However, even with the best intentions of bringing someone relief, any feelings that are either put into a coma or by-passed will wake up someday and escape past all the interventions. Then we'll have to provide the support that should have been supplied from the beginning of our response to a patient's or client's emotional struggling.

Rather than thinking about a patient or telling them, for example, that they are "bipolar and depressed with severe psychotic features while also struggling with an eating disorder," we might be able to see the patient or client as the person they are—and over time—talk with them about the fact that their childhood was emotionally traumatic for them because they:

- were only a child;

- experienced emotional whiplash innumerable times as a child as things went from good or okay to just awful in a nanosecond;

- have a mind and heart that have been working overtime forever; or

- are navigating an eating disorder that might be:
  - how they made or make themself the problem,
  - how they sustained and protected themself, that is, through overeating,
  - how they would symbolically purge themself of all they were emotionally taking in day after day.

A simpler and more empathetic understanding on the part of us helping professionals will make us more effective in what we offer our patients/clients and more humane in how we do it. Even if someone bucks our perspectives, advice, recommendations,

Notes

and even our positive support, their storytelling continues even in these interchanges with us: "Please don't take away from me what I have from my parents and family," or "No one is going to have any control or influence over me because I am going to call all the shots."

How wearying interpretive listening can be. How unrewarding such listening can feel. How difficult it is to be exposed with such regularity to stories of the destruction of our patients'/clients' spirits and peace, the experiences they had endured as children.

However, listening to stories—whether they are shared in conversation or acted out to get them out—is our primary responsibility to our patients and clients. If we do such listening, we'll be able to support those whom we serve as they come to listen to and understand the noise of their own stories. By so doing, they will be freer each day from the hostage-taking nature of these stories. They won't be healed from them, but they will be freer from them, less burdened by them, each day.

> *If we do such listening, we'll be able to support those whom we serve as they come to listen to and understand the noise of their own stories. By doing so, they will be freer each day from the hostage-taking nature of these stories. They won't be healed from them, but they will be freer from them, less burdened by them, each day.*

The unpacking, defrosting, and weeding that lets someone feel freer and less burdened will continue across a lifetime. Staying limber in navigating this dynamic can make all the difference in the world for each of us: for the patient or client, and for ourself, the helping professional, too.

Take care.

Ted

Notes

Last Letter

A Closing Letter to You

Dear Readers:

It has been my privilege to accompany clients who have chosen me to collaborate with them on their brave journey of self-ownership. It's the journey on which we each practice—and as a result get better and better at—living the three-dimensional life that defines what it means to be human, the three dimensions of:

1. managing and enjoying the *PRESENT*,

2. looking to and building the *FUTURE*, and

3. catching and unpacking our earliest *PAST* as it reveals itself through the struggles we experience in life, the defrosted moments of old, childhood pain, the intrusive, false-belief weeds from childhood choking out the garden of who we are today—understanding the truth of what it was like for each of us to be a child.

As we each integrate the processing of our early life experiences into the way we live each day, as we look at and own more of our childhood story, as we come to better understand the ways we worked so very hard emotionally as children—consciously or not—more and more natural flow and peace will arrive in our life.

This is not easy work to do because it truly is learning how to think, feel, and live in a new, brave way. It's learning to navigate the kaleidoscope of who we each are as a human being, a commitment that takes courage to make. When we don't consciously live a three-dimensional life, our life won't be as rich as it could be, and we can unknowingly act out our unpacked, unprocessed pain from childhood on ourself or on others.

When someone is hard on themselves, when someone is hard on someone else, when someone leading a team, group, or company is disrespectful of or abusive to their colleagues: these examples are all the terribly tragic fall-out from how any of these individuals was devalued as a child.

Such acting out of early life pain even happens with leaders of countries and can have national and even global impacts. This happened with the cruel devaluing of the many nations of Indigenous People in North America. It happened in Central and Eastern

Notes

Europe in the 1930s and 40s. It has happened with tragic frequency on the African, Asian, Australian, and South American continents. It happened in Ukraine in 2022.

The greatest injustice is—very simply—not being good to self or others. The greatest justice is achieved from the opposite: being good to self and others. Living one's kaleidoscopic, three-dimensional life responsibly will be the most genuine and generous way to be good to yourself and good to others. If each person just followed the basics of being good to themselves and to others, the world would know quite a different and more pleasant level of peace.

Rather than being a downer or a burden, living our life as a three-dimensional experience will bring us much benefit if we are willing to navigate our life in this way each day. We'll have new energy and agency for living in the present, for building our future, and for unpacking our early life past. It's simply well worth it to make this the way we live.

It's important to remember that this process of three-dimensional, kaleidoscopic living will never end, but when adhered to, the process makes every day better.

> *The process of three-dimensional, kaleidoscopic living will never end, but when adhered to, the process will make every day better.*

Living this process is what lets an *adult* become a *grownup* because it makes each of us responsible to...

- see what we have to see,

- know what we have to know, and

- feel what we have to feel...

... in the present, regarding the future, and from our past, our earliest past.

It can be annoying, for sure, to live a three-dimensional life because including awareness of this third dimension of being human—the impacts of the bafflement and pain from our childhood—means that we have something to manage in life in addition to

---

Notes

being responsible for our present and our future. However, I invite you to live this way because—each day, a little bit more every day—it will bring you an experience of living that feels...

- better,

- clearer,

- lighter,

- freer,

- more fair, and

- more peaceful...

... a life characterized by words ending in *-er*, words that suggest *more* of what we want to experience in life. This process will never be over because it's gentler to us, happening over time, than a blitz of freedom, something our system couldn't handle.

So, because each of us is an amazing person—something that over time we can be humbly grateful for and proud of—we owe it to ourself to chip away each day at the misguided beliefs from childhood that suggest otherwise and that have forever hijacked and "flown our planes" counterproductively, flooding our thoughts and feelings, overwhelming and choking out the essence of who we each are.

Going forward, here are some simple guidelines to integrate into your life. They will help you maintain the energy required to live your three-dimensional life.

Guidelines for Living

1. Eat nutritional foods.

2. Engage in some type of physical activity every day to the degree right for you.

3. Stay paced, measured, rested, respectful of, and gentle with yourself and others.

With the energy harnessed from following these guidelines, you'll be better able to maintain three promises to yourself, to remember three things each day.

Notes

Promises to Self

Promise 1. **Remember that telling the truth is something you owe to yourself.** The biggest truth, the most dismissed, overlooked, brushed-off truth, the most underrated, undervalued, underreported, and undermined truth, and, at times, the most joked-about truth is this:

All moments of emotional bafflement and turmoil experienced in childhood because of a parent and family members:

- were traumatic for the child we each were,

- registered deeply within us, and

- have a lifelong impact.

These experiences are among our first impressions of ourself, of the world, and of life. When these childhood feelings defrost or crop up today, they show us how hard we worked emotionally as children. It requires a lifelong vigilance and effort to diffuse and thus counteract their recurring intrusion into our life.

By way of the struggles that we manage each time they enter our life—struggle being the collision of something today pulling forth a painful moment from childhood stored within us, within our subconscious—we will forever be recovering from the painful bafflements that we experienced when we were children and stored for processing until *later*—which is *now*.

Promise 2. **Remember that your true, natural self is alive and well within you but living in protective custody.** It's waiting to know that your conscious self, your aware self, is attuned to, engaged with, and committed to:

- cleaning up whenever something that was baffling or painful defrosts from your childhood emotional freezer—and pulling every weed from childhood that may crop up,

- releasing long-stored emotional waste and toxins by "going Number 3" through writing with some regularity—just as going Numbers 1 and 2 have some regularity in your life, and

---

Notes

- staying aware that you will feel and may unconsciously live "like the child I once was"—LTCIOW—to one degree or another every day of your life.

As a result, your peaceful, quietly confident, humbly proud, and genuinely alive self will come out of protective custody within you and show up more and more each day—organically so—all on its own.

**Promise 3**. **Remember that being present, living in the moment, is the art and adventure of living a three-dimensional life, the kaleidoscope of what it means to be human.** Whether as the three-dimensional person that you are—or living in a three-dimensional life partnership—the kaleidoscope of navigating the ever-shifting experience of life, of being human is:

- managing and enjoying the PRESENT,

- looking to and building the FUTURE, and

- catching, unpacking, and understanding the PAST, the earliest days of our life—even in utero—whenever our early life stories arrive today at the doorstep of our minds and hearts, arriving costumed as struggle to tell us more hidden truth about what it was like for each of us to be a child.

> _Living in the moment is the art and adventure_
> _of living a three-dimensional life,_
> _the kaleidoscope of what it means to be human._

Maintaining these promises to yourself is what will let the kaleidoscope of life deliver to you:

- the fullness of what it means to be human, and

- the richness of what it means to be YOU.

Your life will flow more and more naturally and effectively. You don't have to live this way, but I believe it will be well worth it if you do.

Notes

All this has been shared with you as we live together in a world that is moving at lightning speed with amazing innovations such as driverless cars and pilotless aircraft. On the terribly concerning side, cybersecurity threats which would impact everyone on the planet are also moving at an incredible pace.

So, as all this innovation—good and bad—progresses, stay true to your most fundamental life responsibility: living your kaleidoscopic, three-dimensional life. It's your most important commitment to yourself. It's the best grounding for life that you can provide yourself. You will know more clearly than ever what you think and feel, what you struggle with, and from where in your life it all comes.

As a client so elegantly said, "It is never too late to see our truth. It is always the right time to feel it and live."

Know that my thoughts, good wishes, and admiration go with you as you choose to engage a forever commitment to living each and every moment of your kaleidoscopic, three-dimensional life—the life that you so deserve—the life that is your birthright to live.

Take care.

Ted

Notes

Appendix A:
Authors of and Resources for Additional Reading

Primary Resources

Jean Jenson
Reclaiming Your Life

Alice Miller
Banished Knowledge
Breaking Down the Wall of Silence
Drama of the Gifted Child (Alice's first book)
For Your Own Good
Free from Lies
Paths of Life
Prisoners of Childhood
The Body Never Lies
The Truth Will Set You Free
The Untouched Key
Thou Shalt Not Be Aware

The United States Centers for Disease Control (CDC)
ACEs (Adverse Childhood Experiences)

Oprah Winfrey and Bruce D. Perry, M.D., Ph.D.
What Happened to You?

Supportive Resources

Peter Breggin
Are Your Prescriptions Killing You?
Psychiatric Drug Withdrawal
Reclaiming Our Children (and more)

Martin Miller
The True Drama of the Gifted Child

Mary Oliver
Dreamwork

M. Scott Peck
People of the Lie
The Road Less Traveled

Robert Whitaker (of *Mad in America*)
Anatomy of an Epidemic

Appendix B:
Meditate through Writing Every Week of the Year

Rather than providing daily suggestions for the meditation that can happen through writing, this is a list of fifty-two writing topics, one for each week of the year. It doesn't matter during which week of a year you start your writing. You don't have to do your writing in the order that these fifty-two topics are presented, nor is it something you have to do every day. Let this simply be writing that you do, reflect on, and build upon week by week with some regularity over the course of a year.

Try to write or print—not fingers to keyboard—three to four times a week for *at least* fifteen minutes each time on that week's meditation. Write whatever comes to mind. Even if you feel stuck, write about that. Remember to use utilitarian paper, that is, a legal pad or spiral notebook, not a journal. Go back to read what you've written, and as you do so, highlight in some way all the words and phrases that jump out at you.

These jump-out words and phrases are things you once experienced and stored. If you had the conscious awareness or skill, you could have written these when you were eighteen years old or younger, most likely when you were still in single digit ages, even in your crib or in your parent's womb. You may want to transfer these into a journal.

Your writing will be a gentle way to grow in personal awareness. As you do so, each week you will more and more be reclaiming your birthright, the birthright of:

> *Living your kaleidoscopic, three-dimensional life,*
> *the richest and fullest experience of being human.*

Week	Meditation
1	The most important job of a parent is to ensure that each child feels good about themselves, safe in the world, confident and peaceful being who they are.
2	What most occupies a child's energy of mind and heart, whether conscious or not, is how to navigate and survive the disappointments and bafflements they're experiencing because of the parent(s) and family they have. This is more critical for a child than academics, sports, or anything else.

Week	Meditation
3	Our two greatest needs as a child are to feel good about ourself and to feel good about our parent(s).
4	Until we become consciously aware, we are driven by the unconscious and unmet needs from our childhood. Until we look at the original drama of our life, we will live variations of it throughout our life.
5	The extent to which we are *at war* in our life today to feel like we matter is the extent to which we were at war as children fighting to matter, fighting to not feel homeless in our own home.
6	When we can't figure out how to be close to a parent or family member, we'll sometimes *wear their behaviors* just as someone would wear a jersey with the number of their most admired athlete.
7	When we don't pull the weeds of false belief when they crop up today, they deplete energy from the garden of who we each are. Sometimes after naming our weeds, we may cling to or get addicted to them because the weeds are a bridge of connection with a parent and our family members. Some people are even comfortable in the hell of these weeds because this hell means being close to a parent and family.
8	Interpreting what someone is acting out is like learning that person's language, thinking in another language. It takes time to become agile at interpreting, deciphering, translating, decoding it—and therefore fluent with it.

Week	Meditation
9	When I'm feeling beside myself, I am beside the self I once was as a child, feeling like the child I once was—LTCIOW— feeling the now-defrosted emotions or cropped-up weeds from that time of my life.
10	Seeing or hearing children can often remind us of what it was like for us to be a child and/or what it wasn't like for us to be a child.
11	When logic doesn't work, there's something that's defrosted from our childhood emotional freezer, or there's a weed of false belief planted in childhood that's cropped up today.
12	Thinking through the impacts of our parent and family members on us is not about blame. It's about understanding emotional dynamics.
13	People who are lost in addictions or some type of personal torture are unconsciously drowning out, smoking out, drugging, diverting from whatever the worst of their childhood pain was. Numbing strategies have often seemed like the only way forward. Someone may unconsciously prefer these strategies so that they can continue evading rather than see, know, and feel their childhood emotional pain.
14	Our greatest loss in childhood often becomes our greatest drive as life proceeds.

Week	Meditation
15	*We were the ones* who unconsciously, instinctively flash froze things in childhood to survive them. Flash freezing is a survival skill in childhood, often an impediment later in life. *Our parents and family members were the ones* who planted the weeds of false beliefs and false presumptions about who we each are, about what we deserve in life, and about what life should and will be like.
16	We are often attracted to and then struggle with people with similarities to a parent or family member and with situations that have similarities to any of the difficult dynamics with which we grew up.
17	A child is terrified when a parent feels like a stranger.
18	When you find yourself running an inner emotional marathon, and when you find yourself lifting heavy loads of truth up and out from within yourself, catch your breath through your mouth, and exhale through your mouth. Do this three or four times. Then step back, go about your day quietly, and "wait for the light bulb of understanding" to come on.
19	Awareness is our best vaccine and our daily booster against any emotional virus that has ever or will ever impact our life. It tones our emotional reflexes to catch what's going on. It strengthens our emotional muscles to hold it as we sort through it.
20	Wear a masking tape bracelet and record a hash mark each time you think or say the word *need*.

Week	Meditation
21	We each live as the person a parent and family members made us to be until our awareness frees us to be otherwise, until we want to be otherwise.
22	Few people were truly safe as children be it physically, sexually, or emotionally. Our brave awareness today can calm the brain and bring the sense that we are safe. The brain can't function well until it is safe.
23	Going back to dig is not necessary. What's ready for unpacking arrives all on its own. Dig/excavate? No. Unpack what shows up? Yes. When things remain boxed up, they remain a heavy burden to carry.
24	True sobriety is being a grownup. Being grownup is: seeing what you have to see, knowing what you have to know, and feeling what you have to feel, especially from your childhood.
25	Children often mirror a parent's actions not because they're learning from the parent but so that the parent can learn from the child and wake up.
26	So often my words are not the words of the moment but the words of my childhood.
27	All of us to some degree drag our childhoods along with us.

Week	Meditation
28	If the biggest impact on us from a parent or family member was a hurtful or negative one, we may unconsciously cuddle with it and want no one to take it away from us.
29	The profound truths that we have to know are there the whole time. We just have to keep rubbing the sleep out of our eyes.
30	The story has been calling my name.
31	I may be holding my breath more than I realize, still trapped in the fear that was mine as a child.
32	A parent's focus has often not been on ensuring that their child feels emotionally comfortable with themself, but rather on making sure their child does nothing to make the parent uncomfortable.
33	Guilt is often a diversion that parks unpleasant "stuff" about others on ourself. Guilt lets us get busy with making ourself the problem when we feel powerless regarding whoever the real problem is. Guilt becomes our safe place, a safe place against great pain.
34	For a child, the message given —in words, actions, attitudes, silences— is the message believed.
35	In the death of false hope comes a lot more believing.

Week	Meditation
36	We are slow to *connect the dots* and/or we *zone out* either in direct proportion to our childhood pain or in direct proportion to the mission of loyalty that we're continuing.
37	To navigate people with emotional viruses of one kind or another, follow the public health measures practiced during the pandemic of 2020-2022: Wear a mask (metaphorically). Social distance. Wash or massage your hands because these interactions are such hard work.
38	We have been busy devaluing ourself.
39	Parents who stay emotionally lazy hurt their children.
40	When the word *need* is not energizing us to engage in something that is truly life and death, it paralyzes us because it makes whatever it is too big, too scary.
41	Remnants of how a parent makes their child feel last forever.
42	Keep the garden weeded, and everything blossoms well. Pull the weeds, and look what shows up all on its own.
43	We carry the memories of baffling childhood experiences deeply in the pockets of our existence.

Week	Meditation
44	The violations against someone's dignity as a child are often cleverly disguised.
45	When anything defrosts from our childhood emotional freezer, it is as raw now as when we first flash froze it.
46	When we regard and treat ourself as a parent and family members regarded and treated us, we do so for two reasons. First, it's dutiful compliance with a false belief of what we deserve in life, of what we are worth. Second, it puts us on the same team as a parent or family member, a desperate way to have a connection with someone where connection has always been elusive.
47	When we were children, we missed nothing going on —nothing— even while still in the womb, our room in the Parent Hotel.
48	When something from our childhood freezer is too difficult to know and feel, we either unconsciously put it on ourself, or we unconsciously put it on someone or something else, even on a food we dislike.
49	Without having conscious awareness, we each continue living—thinking, feeling, and acting— "like the child I once was" (LTCIOW).
50	A parent and family members do not remain the most important people in our lives. However, they forever remain the most impactful.

Week	Meditation
51	Any feeling in life that doesn't make sense, when we don't understand where it's coming from, is some of the old, stored pain that was traumatic for the child we once were. The stored, traumatic, childhood pain has gone nowhere.
52	Living in the moment is the ability to live in the three-dimensional kaleidoscope that every moment is. It's enjoying and managing the present, envisioning and planning the future, unpacking and understanding our childhood past. It's what it means to be human.

www.ingramcontent.com/pod-product-compliance
Lightning Source LLC
Chambersburg PA
CBHW060224030426
42335CB00014B/1338